HOCKEY ADDICT'S GUIDE
NEW YORK CITY

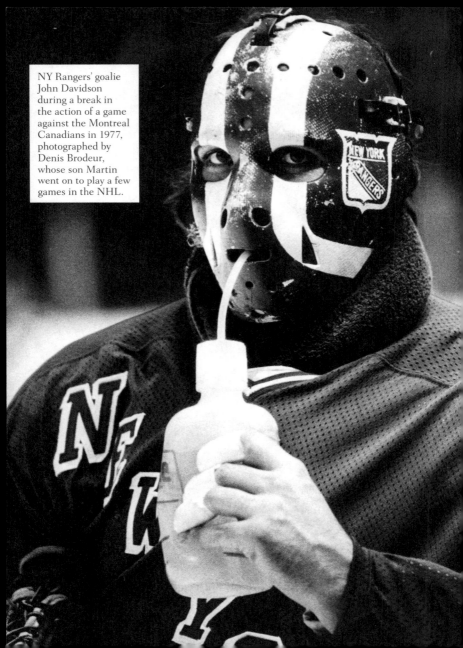

NY Rangers' goalie John Davidson during a break in the action of a game against the Montreal Canadians in 1977, photographed by Denis Brodeur, whose son Martin went on to play a few games in the NHL.

HOCKEY ADDICT'S GUIDE
NEW YORK CITY

WHERE TO EAT, DRINK & PLAY THE ONLY GAME THAT MATTERS

EVAN GUBERNICK

THE COUNTRYMAN PRESS

A division of W. W. Norton & Company

Independent Publishers Since 1923

For information about permission to reproduce selections from this book,
write to Permissions, The Countryman Press, 500 Fifth Avenue, New York, NY 10110

For information about special discounts for bulk purchases, please contact
W. W. Norton Special Sales at specialsales@wwnorton.com or 800-233-4830

Manufacturing by Versa Press

The Countryman Press
www.countrymanpress.com

A division of W. W. Norton & Company, Inc.
500 Fifth Avenue, New York, NY 10110
www.wwnorton.com

978-1-68268-148-0 (pbk.)

10 9 8 7 6 5 4 3 2 1

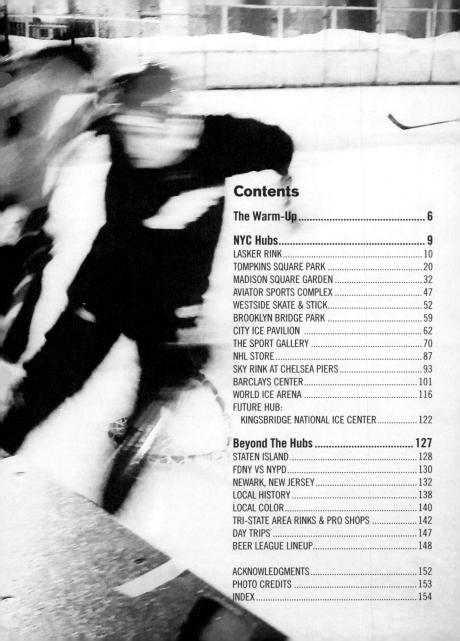

Contents

The Warm-Up

NO CURE EXISTS IF HOCKEY GETS IN YOUR BLOOD. And it's not a seasonal condition, it's a daily obsession. Hourly, even. An obvious symptom: Your life becomes a diversion from hockey, not the other way around. While (relatively) manageable at home, should you venture out of town, you're lost and you know it. Your radar is jammed. Our solution: One city at a time, we're creating a series of guides with recommendations made by those who share your passion for the only sport that matters—including food, drink, lodging, and, of course, where to skate. The guides are a product of local hockey communities, curated, written, and photographed by your fellow puck heads, from fans to beer leaguers, with tips from a few pros sprinkled in. Hockey, at its core, is tribal, connecting us to our cities and to each other, so trust your tribe when you leave your home ice.

————

HOW THE GUIDE IS ORGANIZED Like the game itself, think of this guide as organized chaos. A few set plays off the faceoff, a general gameplan, and then it's on. We've divided the city into "Hubs," must-see places for the hockey-afflicted, and listed additional spots to check out nearby. Think of these recommendations as mini walking tours—and by "walking" we sometimes mean taking the subway or grabbing a Lyft. Your choice. And lastly, we give you a little local hockey history, so if you wind up talking to a local, maybe you'll have a clue. This isn't a typical guidebook. We've avoided the usual ratings, prices, and comparisons. (See Yelp for that.) If it's in here, we like it. We have one map: it's crude, but—like a coach's scribblings—it does its job (sorry, not sorry). Do we miss some obvious hot spots? Probably. Do we lead you down some strange alleys? For sure. But this is a conversation, and we're the only ones talking. If you know of a spot we missed, tell us. Listen, this guide won't solve all your problems. You're still going to have that nightmare where you're sitting on the bench with bare feet. But this guide should help you feel at home in NYC.

————

THE HOCKEY ADDICT'S GUIDE TO NEW YORK CITY Some things you should know: 1) Everything in this city is a 50/50 puck—changing lanes, crossing streets, ordering a beer, reaching for the subway door. And getting ice time. We're here to help. 2) The city is a Rangers city. Every spring, the Blueshirts' crest blooms everywhere, like dandelions. How long they last into the coming heat is a testament to the endless well of hope that only sports can inspire. 3) As Brooklyn solidifies its Left Bank cred, so does the possibility that the Islanders—should they pick a home and grow roots—might one day prove a legit rival if only as the alt choice. We took a leap and included Islanders' legends in the Barclays Hub section because, for now, we can. 4) The Devils? They do have their charm, which comes with their having won more recent Cups than any other local team. 5) As vibrant as the pro scene is, both beer and youth leagues are alive and well, though there's never enough ice in a city of 8.5 million. 6) A few housekeeping notes: In the info we give, the abbreviation NY means Manhattan, BKLYN means Brooklyn, Queens goes by neighborhoods (like the suburb it is). The Bronx gets a mention, and we devote a few pages to Staten Island.

KINGSBRIDGE NATIONAL ICE CENTER

LASKER RINK

MADISON SQUARE
GARDEN

 NHL STORE

 WORLD ICE
ARENA

 CITY ICE PAVILION

SKY RINK
AT CHELSEA PIERS

 WESTSIDE SKATE & STICK

THE SPORT GALLERY

TOMPKINS SQUARE PARK

BROOKLYN BRIDGE PARK

BARCLAYS CENTER

AVIATOR
SPORTS COMPLEX

NYC
Hubs

nyc hub
LASKER RINK
CENTRAL PARK (106TH & 108TH ST.)
917.492.3856

●●●●

Enter Central Park at the north end and walk along East Drive, dodging a menagerie of mobile New Yorkers: runners, cyclists, rollerbladers, speed walkers, dog walkers. Eventually you'll hear the rink before you see it. And even when you do see it, you'll still have to figure out how to reach it, taking a series of awkward paths, until finally, you're there. Two rinks, both undersized, and a building which reeks of . . . authenticity. Home to every age of player and wannabe player, various tournaments, school teams, and charity groups, Lasker, at least while it's cold enough, is very much the hub of outdoor hockey in New York. Constructed in 1966 (making it the oldest hockey facility in the city), the rink is transformed into a swimming pool during the summer, with ice available from late October through March.

ADULT LEAGUES
YOUTH LEAGUES
LOCKER FACILITIES
PRIVATE LESSONS
FOOD COURT

PLAY
PAUL L. McDERMOTT RINK
96TH ST. & 1ST AVE., NY

A new subway line opens up only about once a century, so when the Q line extended service up 2nd Avenue, among the many happy people was the Manhattan Roller League crowd that plays on 1st Avenue and 96th Street, about a five-minute walk from the new stop.

EAT / DRINK
BLONDIES
212 W. 79TH ST., NY • 212.362.4360

If your crew is looking to catch a game and keep the college vibe alive on the UWS, here it is. A throwback sports dive with wall-to-wall screens and no hint of artisanal cocktails, craft beer, or kale chips—just standard pitchers and what some call the best wings around.

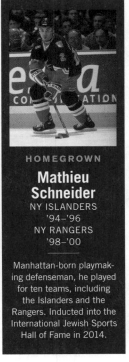

HOMEGROWN
Mathieu Schneider
NY ISLANDERS
'94–'96
NY RANGERS
'98–'00

Manhattan-born playmaking defenseman, he played for ten teams, including the Islanders and the Rangers. Inducted into the International Jewish Sports Hall of Fame in 2014.

EAT / DRINK
CAFE AMRITA
301 W. 110TH ST., NY
212.222.0683

An intimate bar / bistro that doubles as coffee shop / laptop central in daylight hours. The closest place to Lasker for pre-game coffee or post-game beer.

MY PICKS

John Sanful
EXECUTIVE
DIRECTOR,
ICE HOCKEY
IN HARLEM

I grew up in Harlem, and then moved to Brooklyn where I was introduced to hockey. I've been fortunate to channel my passion for the sport as a correspondent for the International Ice Hockey Federation and as Executive Director of Ice Hockey in Harlem.

ALOFT
2296 FREDERICK DOUGLASS BLVD., NY
212.749.4000
1

2

NEIGHBORHOOD
HARLEM (1)
Enjoy the new Harlem renaissance. Harlem is the cultural capital of Black America. With decades of history ever-present, Harlem also boasts some of the best restaurants, bars, and cultural institutions in the country. Find a restaurant on Frederick Douglass Boulevard, visit the Apollo, and stay at Aloft.

EAT
STREETBIRD ROTISSERIE (2)
2149 FREDERICK DOUGLASS BLVD., NY
212.206.2557
Marcus Samuelsson's "chicken joint" in Harlem is a cozy place for elevated poultry dishes and old-school hip-hop. The Crispy Bird sandwich is unforgettable.

BEYOND THE HUB

EAT / DRINK
COOPER'S CRAFT & KITCHEN
169 8TH AVE., NY
646.661.7711
I enjoy a very good craft beer, and Cooper's Craft & Kitchen has some of the best on tap and excellent small bites to boot.

MUSIC VENUE
CITY WINERY
155 VARICK ST., NY • 212.608.0555
The only place I can enjoy a smooth Merlot while seeing Christopher Cross put on an intimate show. The venue has great sight lines, whether you're sitting at the bar, a high-top table, or near the stage.

POOL
SLATE NY
54 W. 21ST ST., NY • 212.989.0096
This Flatiron District gem is where I met my wife. Two floors and 16,000 square feet, SLATE has good food, drinks, and pool tables on the lower level.

COMIC BOOKS
FORBIDDEN PLANET(3)
832 BROADWAY, NY • 212.473.1576
As a collector of comic books, Forbidden Planet is my place. Whether I'm looking for the latest Civil War series, or Frank Miller's best work outside of *Sin City* and *Batman Returns*, Forbidden City does not disappoint. The sales staff is knowledgeable and patient.

GYM
BLINK
MULTIPLE LOCATIONS
You can't go wrong with Blink. It's affordable, and you can get a good workout.

DAY TRIP
STORM KING ART CENTER
1 MUSEUM RD., NEW WINDSOR, NY 845.534.3115
A favorite. For fifty years, Storm King Art Center has featured exhibits from artists and sculptors in a serene lower Hudson Valley setting. Taking a walk through the park, you'll find many wonderful creations. On a beautiful spring or summer day, Storm King Art Center is a calm, hopeful, and peaceful place to visit.

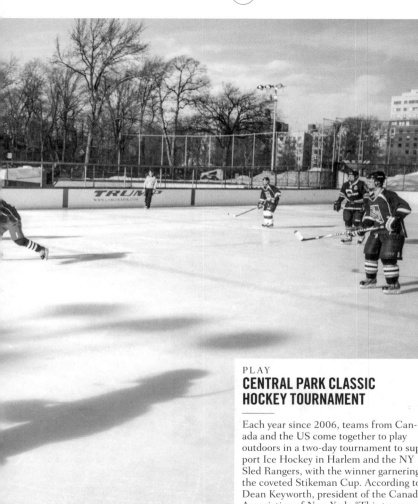
PLAY

CENTRAL PARK CLASSIC HOCKEY TOURNAMENT

Each year since 2006, teams from Canada and the US come together to play outdoors in a two-day tournament to support Ice Hockey in Harlem and the NY Sled Rangers, with the winner garnering the coveted Stikeman Cup. According to Dean Keyworth, president of the Canadian Association of New York, "This tournament is intended to further the natural ties between Canadians and New Yorkers." But let's be honest: Our northern neighbors will always be much nicer than us.

EAT / DRINK
HARLEM TAVERN
2153 FREDERICK DOUGLASS BLVD., NY • 212.866.4500

Large outdoor beer garden with a solid beer list, including Harlem Blue Hectic, a smooth local IPA named for "Hectic Harlem," Roi Ottley's column in the historic newspaper *The Amsterdam News*.

EAT / DRINK
MANNY'S ON SECOND
1770 2ND AVE., NY • 212.410.3300

If your Airbnb is a tiny uptown studio, this place will probably become your living room. Surrounded by 20+ screens, you'll be happy with their standard bar fare, fine tap selection, and private party room upstairs for you and your closest 100 friends. You get the feeling they might even let you leave your gear here (never hurts to ask). A touch of real on the UES (Upper East Side).

MY PICKS
Stan Fischler
BROADCASTER

EAT
LA PICCOLA CUCINA
964 AMSTERDAM AVE., NY
212.866.1336
Northern Italian bistro run by a Mexican chef.

V & T
1024 AMSTERDAM AVE., NY
212.663.1708
My favorite waiter, Marc from Serbia, is a huge Islander fan.

THE MANCHESTER DINER
2800 BROADWAY, NY
212.665.7712
Used to be called a luncheonette, now it's a diner.

HANG
CROWN MACHINE SERVICES
2792 BROADWAY, NY
They fix everything: sewing machines, vacuum cleaners, typewriters—you name it. Run by two big Ranger fans. Every year I assure them the Rangers are going to win the Cup.

BARBERSHOP
SAMMY'S BARBER SHOP
926 AMSTERDAM AVE., NY
Russian barber, always knows exactly what I want.

PLAY
RIVERBANK STATE PARK ICE RINK
HENRY HUDSON PKWY
BETWEEN W. 138TH &
W. 145TH ST., NY
212.694.3642

Ice hockey in the winter (November to March) and roller for the rest of the year, with clinics, leagues, and open availability for all age groups.

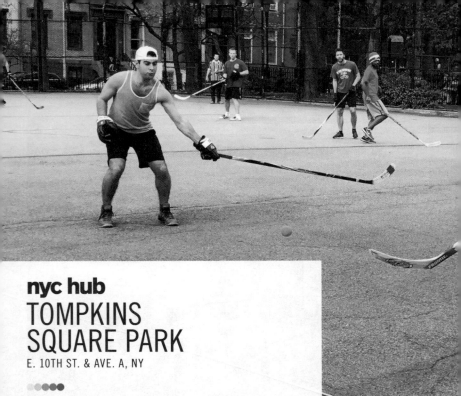

nyc hub
TOMPKINS
SQUARE PARK
E. 10TH ST. & AVE. A, NY

●●●●●

Riot, protest, and general conflict have always been at home in
Tompkins Square Park, from 19th-century workers' strikes to the
more recent police crackdowns on tent-city encampments. The
tempestuous energy of this neighborhood persists, albeit with a
touch of irony and gig-life ennui, and since 2000, the park has been
home to Blacktop Street Hockey (BTSH). According to its founder,
hockey was the perfect sport for the neighborhood crowd, requir-
ing "very little athletic skill, but a lot of pent up aggression and
hatred." The players, who currently gather on Sundays from late
March through October, comprising 20 teams in all, might debate
the level of skill required, but their smiles and camaraderie do a
fine job of masking what must surely be deep and intense enmity.

EAT
ECONOMY CANDY
108 RIVINGTON ST., NY
212.254.1531

If you didn't know better, you might assume this to be the exact type of spot—old school logo, interior from another era (selling . . . candy?)—to be replaced by a nail salon or espresso bar. But here's a secret: Candy = childhood = nostalgia, which never goes out of style. Your lizard brain, with sugar at its core, is already mapping a route.

EAT
KATZ'S DELICATESSAN
205 E. HOUSTON ST., NY
212.254.2246

Jon Merrill
VEGAS GOLDEN
KNIGHTS
'17–PRESENT
NJ DEVILS '13–'17

EAT
KATZ'S DELI
205 E. HOUSTON ST., NY
212.254.2246

SUGARFISH
33 E. 20TH ST., NY
347.705.8100

TAQUERIA DOWNTOWN
236 GROVE ST., JERSEY CITY, NJ
201.333.3220

The scent of meat, especially of the cured variety, speaks to your carnivorous self. Katz's selling its air rights to a neighboring lot being developed won't stop the wafting primal aroma from intoxicating both locals and tourists.

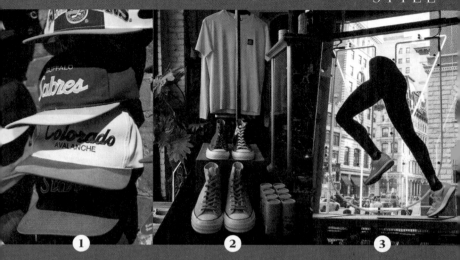

(1) (2) (3)

VINTAGE
MISTER THROWBACK (1)
428 E. 9TH ST., NY • 646.410.0310
Most fun vintage shop in NYC and as welcoming as can be. Endless nostalgia pieces, from hockey jerseys to video games to wrestling toys. If you're old enough to remember, you'll feel like you're back in your childhood bedroom.

PROCELL
5 DELANCEY ST., NY • 212.226.2315
Specializes in the rarest vintage pieces, a really eclectic mix that attracts a who's who of New York City sneaker-fashion-design-culture

WRITTEN & CURATED BY JASON FAUSTINO

aficionados. Stylists for high-profile celebrities shop here to find rare, one-of-a-kind items, like a 1997 Wu-Tang Clan / Rage Against the Machine tour shirt for $400.

APPAREL
KINFOLK (2)
90 WYTHE AVE., BKLYN
347.689.4939
Doubles as a brand and a bar. A really cool private label— they sell their own apparel and accessories, graphic tees, bikes, and a lot more.

NOAH
195 MULBERRY ST., NY
Brand / retail spot founded by former creative director of Supreme. Sophisticated hype, equal parts Japanese influence and Americana.

NIKE RUNNING FLATIRON (3)
156 5TH AVE., NY • 212.243.8560
They specialize in running, so all of the new associated technology and platforms debut here. Running groups leave out of here, so if you're trying to sneak in a run while you're in NYC, you can probably catch one that leaves out of Nike Flatiron.

JEWELRY
THE GREAT FROG
72 ORCHARD ST., NY • 646.370.5727
Eclectic jewelry for anyone who's into rings, necklaces, etc., both men's and women's.

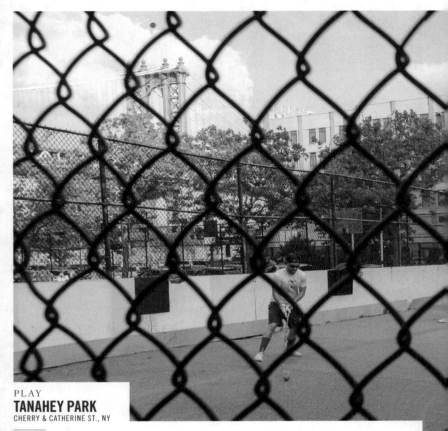

PLAY
TANAHEY PARK
CHERRY & CATHERINE ST., NY

Along the East River, sandwiched between Chinatown and the LES (Lower East Side), sits a neighborhood few New Yorkers or Uber drivers have ever heard of called Two Bridges. The bridges, Brooklyn and Manhattan, are both visible from yet another secret place: a full-on street hockey rink, with boards, benches, and everything else needed for actual, official matches, which is why two organized leagues (Mofo and the aptly, if unimaginatively, named Two Bridges) call this rink home. The games are, for the most part, collegial: fighting isn't tolerated, contact is discouraged, and sticks are kept down below the knee, but the pace still tends toward the frantic. This enclosed rink is a dream to all who have ever played in the usual urban setting, where you spend most of your time retrieving the ball from surrounding, if not oncoming, traffic.

BEER
LEAGUE
PICK
MIKHAIL BORTNIK*

APPAREL
EXTRA BUTTER
125 ORCHARD ST., NY
917.965.2500

A great place to get
your fill on clothes and
shoes. They get all the
limited sneaker releases
and have a great eye
for curation---mixing
streetwear, contemporary
brands, and those things
that fit along the edges.

VINTAGE
METROPOLIS
43 3RD AVE., NY
212.358.0795

I've been coming to this
East Village mainstay since
I was in high school. If this
shop ever closes, I'll cry.
Two floors of immaculately
curated vintage clothing,
from sportswear to band
tees. They're always on top
of the trends.

* HONORARY BEER LEAGUER

VINYL
A1 RECORD SHOP
439 E. 6TH ST., NY
212.473.2870

A crate-digging mecca, this
flea-market booth turned
brick-and-mortar has been
buying and selling seven
days a week for over 20
years, long before the current vinyl boom.

BEER
LEAGUE
PICK
JASON FAUSTINO

MOVIES
METROGRAPH
7 LUDLOW ST., NY
212.660.0312
Pretty new, right in the
heart of the Lower East
Side. Very boutique, very
curated as well—they
pick films that tell a good
story. Amazing candy
concession stand.

EAT
SWEET CHICK
178 LUDLOW ST., NY
646.657.0233

This LES location of the Williamsburg original features
the standard (and spectacular) chicken and waffles, along
with $12 hip-hop-inspired cocktails (try the Christopher
Wallace—five-year aged rum, blended scotch, maple syrup,
and whiskey barrel-aged bitters). Additional cred comes
courtesy of co-owner, Mr. Nasir Jones.

ICE CREAM
TAIYAKI
119 BAXTER ST., NY
212.966.2882

Trust me when I say you will never look at ice cream the same way after you've had this deliciousness inside Taiyaki's warm, soft, fish-shaped waffle cone. You won't be able to eat it fast enough! (Literally, because the ice cream will start melting super fast since all their waffle cones are made fresh as soon as they are ordered.)

EAT
VESELKA
144 2ND AVE., NY
212.228.9682

Ukrainian, family-owned, open 24 hours (remember that). Eat fast so you won't be late for your nap.

PLAY
THE ICE AT STUYTOWN
PLAYGROUND 10, STUYVESANT TOWN, NY

The good news: There's an outdoor rink in the East Village which, during winter months, has open hockey on Saturday mornings and youth hockey clinics three times a week. The bad news: The rink is open only to tenants of the apartment complex and their guests, not the general public. So here are your choices: 1) Sign a lease (a recent StreetEasy listing had a 745 sq. ft. one bedroom for $3,270). 2) Show up with your gear plus some donuts and make a friend.

DRINK
COUP
64 COOPER SQ., NY
212.260.2182

Politics, along with other hot-button topics, are hinted at but rarely openly discussed in the locker room. Not only is the mix of political views a wide one, it's also passionate and short-fused (hence: hockey). Which brings us to this openly political spot where 20 bucks buys you a drink, including tax, tip, and a donation to a revolving selection of non-profits whose funding is being threatened by the current administration. Drinks are simple and strong at this pop-up, whose plan is to remain open until at least 2020.

MY PICKS

Calvin Burkhart

NYU GOALIE

Calvin Burkhart has been playing hockey for nearly 20 years, though he has been a New Yorker for only one. His interests include writing, directing, playing guitar and video games, and writing short biographies in the third person.

EAT

WO HOP CITY [1]

15 MOTT ST., NY
212.566.3841

This Mott Street staple has been serving up your favorite Cantonese dishes since 1938. Here, you're not just tasting one of Chinatown's oldest and best, you're having a hefty serving of history.

COCORON NOODLES

16 DELANCEY ST., NY
212.477.1212

Hit up this well-located Japanese restaurant (nestled right between Bowery Ballroom and Sara D. Roosevelt Park) for some of the best Soba noodles in the city.

Step inside for a feel of Tokyo before heading back out into the heart of New York.

LAM ZHOU HANDMADE NOODLE

144 E. BROADWAY, NY
212.566.6933

As with many of these holes-in-the-wall along East Broadway, be warned: If you're not fluent in Mandarin, be ready for a study in communication. But the dumplings (8/$3) speak for themselves. This place might be no-frills, but it's one of the best values in the city for absolutely incredible homemade noodles and dumplings.

CHEEKY'S

35 ORCHARD ST., NY
646.504.8132

NYC generally favors pastrami over po'boys, but don't let that dissuade you from trying this NOLA-themed sandwich shop. Just past the eastern edge of Chinatown, Cheeky's brings a hell of a sandwich to what is becoming one of the trendiest parts of downtown.

2

DRINK
WHISKEY TAVERN
79 BAXTER ST., NY • 212.374.9119
Across from the city jail and just north of Columbus Park, and equally suited to patrons headed to either. If seeking a respectable whiskey list and a blue-collar vibe, you'll find no better around these parts.

MR. FONG'S (2)
40 MARKET ST., NY
You might miss this bar amidst the wafts of fish and the rumble of subway cars over the Manhattan Bridge.

Don't bother looking for the sign, there isn't one; but once you're inside, you'll find it's literally and figuratively a breath of fresh air. An oasis from typical LES bros: a broasis?

DESSERT
10BELOW
10 MOTT ST., NY • 646.861.2040
10Below seeks to bring the kind of artisanal precision to its Thai-inspired ice cream that many Chinatown restaurants have been adopting in their menus. A perfect des-

sert after one of the numerous amazing restaurants along Mott Street. This stuff isn't just another Facebook video fad.

ERIN MCKENNA'S BAKERY
248 BROOME ST., NY • 855.462.2292
If you're looking for the best gluten-free bread, pastries, and cupcakes, but you don't find yourself walking distance to Disneyworld or LA (the sites of this bakery's two other locations), this is your spot.

BEER LEAGUE PICK
BRIAN CURTIN

DRINK
NIAGARA
112 AVE. A, NY
212.420.9517

You can always count me in for cheap drinks in a cool neighborhood. Add in a mural of The Clash frontman Joe Strummer and a photo booth, and you have yourself a good dive bar.

DRINK
WILLIAM BARNACLE TAVERN
80 ST. MARKS PLACE, NY

The Green Fairy, more commonly known as absinthe, benefits from its reputation as a hallucinogen, one which can supposedly help with the writing of your novel (or travel guide). A favorite of both Picasso and *New Girl*, this spirit is a featured player at this Prohibition-era nook attached to Theatre 80 St. Marks.

APPAREL
COMMUNITY 54
186 AVE. B, NY
212.673.7060

"Clothing, community, culture" is the three-word mantra of this LES boutique, named in honor of Studio 54, the iconic mecca of '70s fame. The store features the usual menu of kicks, tees, hoodies, and knick knacks, featuring a diverse array of brands, along with the obligatory arcade games, photo booth, and art gallery.

SAN MARCO PIZZERIA
577 LORIMER ST., BKLYN
718.387.4861

$2.50/plain slice. Basic, nothin' to write home about. Simple. This joint has been here since 1969. Cool.

ROEBLING PIZZA
326 ROEBLING ST., BKLYN
718.782.5042

GREAT ol' hole-in-da-wall joint has been around since 1960. Stiff-n-tasty crust, good sauce, oily cheese, but whatever. Hot sauce rim was a mistake, though.

SLICE PIZZERIA
48–11 VERNON BLVD., LIC
718.937.5423

$3.25/margherita slice. Beauty of a slice in #long-islandcity @slice_lic. Fresh, simple sauce with a very good crust and quality cheese.

PRONTO PIZZA
114 LIBERTY ST., NY
212.374.9595

$3.50/eggplant slice. Fried in old burnt oil for tourists, construction workers, office workers, and me.

WRITTEN & CURATED BY JACK CHINELLI

FAMOUS FAMIGLIA
757 BROADWAY, NY
212.353.2900

$4.67/grandma-special slice. Italian-themed chain run by Albanians from the former Yugoslavia bossing around Hispanic dudes. ¯_( )_/¯. S'ok, dried oregano overdose, passable crust.

JOE'S PIZZA
216 BEDFORD AVE., BKLYN
718.388.2216

$2.75/plain slice. One plain slice, please. Good job on the sauce today @joespizzanyc.

nyc hub
MADISON SQUARE GARDEN

4 PENNSYLVANIA PLAZA, NY • 212.465.6741

Living in NYC, we take icons for granted. We walk by the Chrysler Building without looking up. We see Julia Roberts hailing a cab and we think, "There's Julia Roberts hailing a cab." Same goes for MSG. We rush to the game, grab a beer, and find our seat, rarely pausing . . . to look around. If you can forget for a moment the Dolans, the dearth of Cups, and the train station the Garden sits on top of, the space itself is breathtaking, enhanced in 2013 by a billion-dollar facelift. The accompanying photograph makes description redundant but, fan or not, a trip here is a must. Tickets aren't cheap, and the level of passion from the crowd seems to rise according to distance from the ice. But history does count for something, even if this particular edition of the Garden dates back only (!) to 1968. Of course, many of the moments whose ghosts haunt these aisles have nothing to do with hockey: the Ali/Frazier fight, the Concert for New York City after the 9/11 attack, Billy Joel, and—the one you're all thinking about—the annual Westminster Kennel Club Dog Show.

- ONLY ARENA CEILING IN THE WORLD THAT IS CONCAVE, RATHER THAN CONVEX
- LOCKER ROOMS ARE ROUND, FORCING ALL PLAYERS TO FACE EACH OTHER, A REMINDER OF THEIR SHARED RESPONSIBILITY
- NO ONE STEPS ON THE LOGO ON THE FLOOR OF THE LOCKER ROOM

PLAY
ROBERT MOSES PLAYGROUND
FIRST AVE. & 42ND ST., NY
212.753.0198

The East End Hockey Association has organized roller play at this location for almost 50 years, enlisting even Moses himself (Robert, that is) to pen a letter of support for the playground when a developer wanted to rip it up and construct a building in its place. Ironic, since Moses was a famous urban planner renowned for tearing up anything in his way to build an astounding number of roads and bridges in the Metro area. On the bright side, he was instrumental in bringing the UN (background) to the city. The group pictured here puts on a nice show on Saturday mornings, weather permitting.

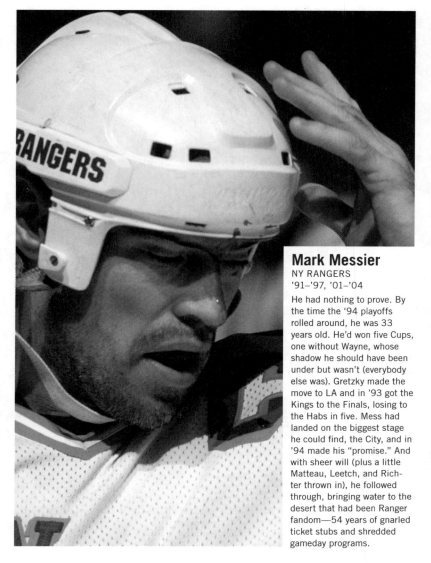

Mark Messier
NY RANGERS
'91–'97, '01–'04

He had nothing to prove. By the time the '94 playoffs rolled around, he was 33 years old. He'd won five Cups, one without Wayne, whose shadow he should have been under but wasn't (everybody else was). Gretzky made the move to LA and in '93 got the Kings to the Finals, losing to the Habs in five. Mess had landed on the biggest stage he could find, the City, and in '94 made his "promise." And with sheer will (plus a little Matteau, Leetch, and Richter thrown in), he followed through, bringing water to the desert that had been Ranger fandom—54 years of gnarled ticket stubs and shredded gameday programs.

MY PICKS

Paul Curtis
ZAMBONI DRIVER,
MADISON SQUARE
GARDEN

How'd you get the job? I was working here as a Local 3 utility worker—one of the guys was retiring, and they asked if I wanted to take his place. Been on the ice since 2000. **Is it a sought-after gig?** It is and it isn't. A lot of work, a big time commitment. You miss a lot of family events. **Is it complicated?** Difficult at first, but with practice I've got a hell of a lot better at it. **How about those kids you have to drive around?** You get the odd hyper one, but usually they're so in awe of the whole thing. **What do you do in the off-season?** Build a stage, drive a forklift, anything they ask me. **Ever play hockey?** Tried, but I can't skate. I'm terrible at it. Fell over on my head a few times. **Where are you from?** London, England. **Ever forget which side of the ice to drive on**? Clever.

EAT
VILLA MOSCONI
69 MACDOUGAL ST., NY
212.673.0390
Great Italian restaurant, really lovely people, got to know them over the years. If it's not on the menu, they'll still cook it for you. I do recommend a carafe of the house red.

ARTURO'S
106 W. HOUSTON ST., NY
212.677.3820
Great pizza. An Asian woman playing Broadway show tunes on a baby grand. Arturo was the world's worst artist. There's a painting of Sea Biscuit, looks no more like a horse than I do.

DRINK
FOOTBALL FACTORY AT LEGENDS
6 W. 33RD ST., NY
212.967.7792
Go and watch real football. My team is the Queens Park Rangers. They're why I started supporting the NY Rangers when I first got here.

SLEEP
Z NYC HOTEL (1)
11-01 43RD AVE., LIC
212.319.7000
Nice boutique hotel. Quick, easy trip to midtown, but nice enough to keep you in LIC.

Matteau Matteau Matteau
MAY 27, 1994

No Richter, Leetch, Graves, Gilbert, Bathgate, or Giacomin, but we run a photo of Matteau, and Ranger fans know why. Without this awkward, ugly duckling of a goal (his second overtime winner of the series), the faithful might still be hearing "1940" rain down from crowds coast to coast. True, a seven-game series with the Canucks still had to be won, but this double-overtime squeaker past a stunned rookie named Brodeur ended the Eastern Conference Finals and ensured the Cup was destined to be driven down Broadway in a shower of shredded paper, all of which led to a nice overtime check for members of the Sanitation Department, who were smiling for two reasons.

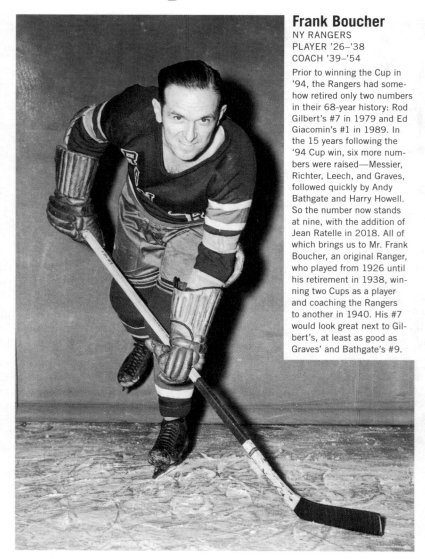

Frank Boucher

NY RANGERS
PLAYER '26–'38
COACH '39–'54

Prior to winning the Cup in '94, the Rangers had somehow retired only two numbers in their 68-year history: Rod Gilbert's #7 in 1979 and Ed Giacomin's #1 in 1989. In the 15 years following the '94 Cup win, six more numbers were raised—Messier, Richter, Leech, and Graves, followed quickly by Andy Bathgate and Harry Howell. So the number now stands at nine, with the addition of Jean Ratelle in 2018. All of which brings us to Mr. Frank Boucher, an original Ranger, who played from 1926 until his retirement in 1938, winning two Cups as a player and coaching the Rangers to another in 1940. His #7 would look great next to Gilbert's, at least as good as Graves' and Bathgate's #9.

EAT
MANDOO BAR
2 W. 32ND ST., NY • 212.279.3075

Watch your pre-game dumplings get prepared before you even sit down. Fast, cheap, and a seven-minute walk to the Garden. Perfect combination of carb and protein, and a fine absorbant of libations to follow.

MUSIC
THE CUTTING ROOM
44 E. 32ND ST., NY • 212.691.1900

Originally situated in the Garment District (hence the name), this multi-genre performance space, co-founded by actor Christopher Noth of Mr. Big fame, moved to its current locale in 2013.

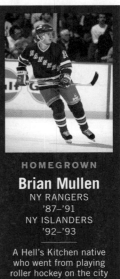

HOMEGROWN
Brian Mullen
NY RANGERS
'87–'91
NY ISLANDERS
'92–'93

A Hell's Kitchen native who went from playing roller hockey on the city streets to suiting up for both the hometown teams.

BUY
GERRY COSBY
11 PENNSYLVANIA PLAZA, NY
212.563.6464

Founded by Gerry Cosby, a NY Rover goaltender, and formerly located on the ground floor at MSG. "Let's meet in front of Cosby's" was a common suggestion, back in the day, and somehow 18,200 fans (MSG's pre-renovation capacity) could rendezvous in one place and all find their seat buddies by puck drop.

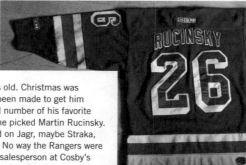

"IT'S SPELLED R-U-C-I-N-S-K-Y"

The kid was eight, maybe nine years old. Christmas was approaching, and the decision had been made to get him a Rangers jersey, with the name and number of his favorite player. For reasons unknown to us, he picked Martin Rucinsky. We spent weeks trying to sell the kid on Jagr, maybe Straka, but nope, his favorite was Rucinsky. No way the Rangers were selling even a Rucinsky T-shirt. The salesperson at Cosby's was a bit incredulous as well, double-checking the spelling as he wrote the order. That Christmas was, to that point, the greatest day in the kid's life, and Rucinsky's as well, though he probably didn't know it. We'd put the jersey on eBay, but our guess is there'd be only one bid.

Boston Bruins
vs NY Rangers
DECEMBER 29, 1973

With the Rangers' goalie pulled, Gerry Cheevers stops Phil Esposito on a breakaway seconds before the buzzer. The Bruins win, and, unremarkably, the two teams linger on the ice, with the usual shoving and bad language. But as the simmering group moved towards the boards, the Bruins' Terry O'Reilly, never the pacifist, remarkably hurtles the partition and attacks a Rangers fan like, well, like a bear escaping his pen at the zoo. Apparently, the fan had grabbed a stick from one of the Bruins and had started hitting O'Reilly and his teammates as they remained on the ice. A total of 18 Bruins climbed their way into the seats, including Mike Milbury who accosted a fan with his own shoe ("I didn't hit him in the head"). The irony is Milbury had already gone to the locker room, only to wonder where the rest of his team was, then upon returning to the ice, saw half of them in the stands. What the Rangers were thinking as they watched this mayhem unfold in front of them remains a mystery.

Jean Ratelle

NY RANGERS '61–'75

Smooth skating, slick passing, consistent aim, the only question might be why it took over forty years to throw his number on a flag and hang it in the Garden. Rumor has it there was a bit of bad blood with the Blueshirts since Ratelle finished his career as a Bruin, and continued working with that organization after his retirement. OK, how did he wind up in Beantown? Uhh, he got traded. And neither team kissed the Cup as a result. Maybe the NY higher-ups were waiting to see which jersey he picked to represent him when he was selected one of the NHL 100 Greatest. It was the Rangers.

ISLANDERS
OFFSIDE TAVERN [1]
137 W. 14TH ST., NY
917.388.3956

An Islanders' bar? In Manhattan? They're on the wrong side of the bridge! Well, believe it or not, Offside Tavern is Manhattan's only official Mike Bossy fan club. But with a projection room, private TV tables, free buttered popcorn, and Mario Kart Mondays, this place has enough to tame even the rowdiest of the Rangers' faithful. Like the best sports bars, Offside has a habit of sucking time out of the air, so tell your loved ones not to stay up waiting.

WRITTEN &
CURATED BY
DANNY
BLANDA

RANGERS
FLYING PUCK
364 7TH AVE., NY
212.736.5353

Heavy wooden doors, stained glass windows, and nostalgic hockey murals, this bar is a Rangers Cathedral. And quite like a cathedral, be prepared to donate to "the offering plate." Let's put it this way, if you can afford a Rangers ticket, this is the bar for you (the Flying Puck "doesn't do happy hour").

SHARKS
FINNERTY'S
221 2ND AVE., NY
212.677.2655

Finnerty's is a California transplant bar with too much ease for West Coast's restless tectonics. This Dude-Abiding bar is home base for all Bay Area sports, including the San Jose Sharks. A socially acceptable, sun-soaked,

day-drinking location that rents out tables equipped with their own personal taps and keg service. So whether you're celebrating a birthday, a bar mitzvah, or a friend's sobriety, this is the place to plan an event. Call ahead.

BRUINS
PROFESSOR THOM'S
219 2ND AVE., NY
212.260.9480

Boston! Beer! Bells! Booths! And Boston! This two-story spot has everything Beantown, from Gronk-O's to Lobster Mondays! If Boston scores, in any sport, the bartenders ring a bell to let you know. This is THE Boston stronghold of New York, and if you're a Bruins fan, you'll feel at home when over 150 religious Bostonians all come out to yell at the TVs during the playoffs. They're even wicked nice to outsiders, unless you're a New York fan.

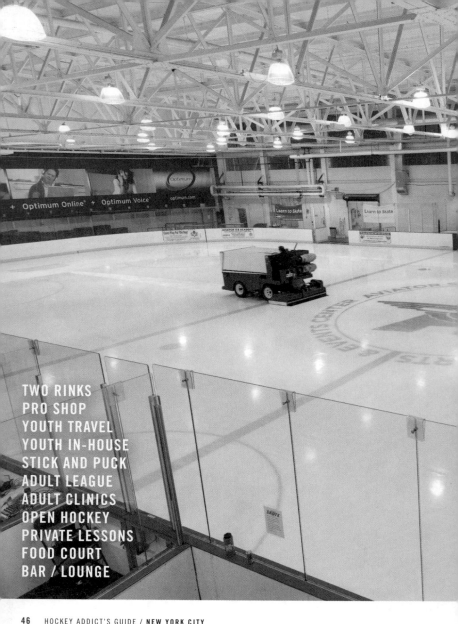

TWO RINKS
PRO SHOP
YOUTH TRAVEL
YOUTH IN-HOUSE
STICK AND PUCK
ADULT LEAGUE
ADULT CLINICS
OPEN HOCKEY
PRIVATE LESSONS
FOOD COURT
BAR / LOUNGE

nyc hub
AVIATOR SPORTS COMPLEX
3159 FLATBUSH AVE., BKLYN
718.758.7500

●●●●

Retro-fitting aircraft hangers into two NHL-sized ice rinks was inspired thinking, but since they sit within a Gateway National Recreation Area, a few house rules are in order: 1) In the case of a government shutdown, the rinks won't be open (been there), and 2) After a late-night beer league game, stay in the locker room with your beverage and tall tales, since lingering in the parking lot past the witching hour is technically against the law, as a Park Ranger will be happy to inform you (check). Opened in 2006 as Brooklyn's only year-round ice, Aviator Sports and Events Center offers more than just the two rinks. They've also got basketball, soccer, and rock-climbing facilties—and one of the more entertaining thrill rides in the city is driving down Flatbush Avenue toward Jamaica Bay, with all the "dollar vans" and questionable lane maneuvers, to arrive at Floyd Bennett Field, NYC's first airport. Finding your way to the rinks, you'll be rambling down the same runway as Amelia Earhart, Howard Hughes, Douglas "Wrong Way" Corrigan, and John Glenn. More good news: Parking is free and there's plenty of it.

CONEY ISLAND

HANG
THE BOARDWALK

The crowd changes as the sun sets, with happy families giving way, sometimes frantically, to a more eclectic array of characters.

VENUE
FORD AMPHITHEATER

A 5,000-seat covered open-air venue, the exterior of which incorporates the landmark 1923 Childs Building.

ACTIVITY
RIDES

The Parachute Jump is defunct, but check out lunaparknyc.com, where the rides are categorized by level of thrill.

WATCH
MCU PARK

Home to the New York Mets' minor-league affiliate, the A-level Brooklyn Cyclones.

EAT
NATHAN'S FAMOUS

Do not, repeat DO NOT, watch their annual hot-dog-eating contest if you ever plan to sample the goods.

BEACHES OF NEW YORK CITY (YES, WE'RE ON THE OCEAN)

BROOKLYN
**BRIGHTON BEACH
CONEY ISLAND
MANHATTAN BEACH**

THE BRONX
ORCHARD BEACH

QUEENS
**ROCKAWAY BEACH
FORT TILDEN BEACH
JACOB RIIS PARK BEACH**

STATEN ISLAND
**CEDAR GROVE BEACH
MIDLAND BEACH
SOUTH BEACH
WOLFE'S POND BEACH**

PLAY
ABE STARK
CONEY ISLAND BOARDWALK & W. 19TH ST., BKLYN
718.946.3135

Check out old newsreel footage from Ebbets Field, and there's a good chance you'll see a sign in the outfield: "Hit Sign, Win Suit." A clever out-of-home ad stunt by Abe Stark, owner of a clothing shop on Pitkin Avenue in the Brownsville neighborhood of Brooklyn, who later went on to become borough president of Brooklyn. If these details conjure images of old New York, then so will the ice rink on the Coney Island boardwalk which bears Stark's name. Home to the New York Stars, Mite through Midget, the rink is open to the public on weekends, October through March, though it only seems right that the rink should remain open for hockey in the summer, considering that the Coney Island Polar Bear Club, "the oldest winter bathing organization in the US," gathers a unique crowd each winter to jump in the freezing ocean, only steps away from the ice.

YOUTH HOUSE LEAGUE
YOUTH TRAVEL
SKATING LESSONS

EAT
UMA'S
92-07 ROCKAWAY BEACH BLVD.
FAR ROCKAWAY
718.318.9100

Located on an up-and-coming stretch of the Rockaways, this spot serves up large portions of the authentic, hearty cuisine of landlocked Uzbekistan. Opened the year after Hurricane Sandy rolled through, it's become a hub for the local surfing crowd.

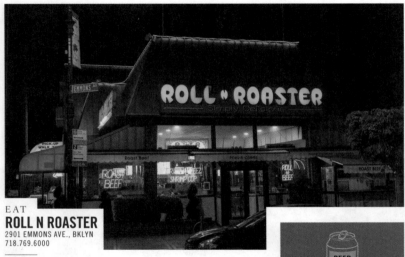

EAT
ROLL N ROASTER
2901 EMMONS AVE., BKLYN
718.769.6000

It's about midnight, and we've wasted enough time in the postgame locker room avoiding a return to our regular lives, when some brilliant mind shouts an inspired command, "We're going to Roll N Roaster." They shut down at 1 a.m. most nights, so it's a bit of an ugly shuffle to our cars, but soon enough we snake out of the Aviator parking lot, some of us knowing the way, some not. Like a funeral procession running late, we hop on the Belt Parkway, turn off at the Sheepshead Bay exit, and look to park, en masse, in front of a restaurant that appears to have been designed by whoever worked on the Brady Bunch house (entirely possible since they're both from the '70s). Their speciality is a roast beef sandwich with some cheesy gravy fries, but frankly it's all a drunken carb / protein hallucination, the last frame of which involves catching sight of the bottom item on the enormous wall-mounted menu: a bottle of Moet Champagne for about sixty bucks. And by then, it makes complete sense.

BEER
LEAGUE
PICK
BRIAN CURTIN

EAT
BRENNAN & CARR
3432 NOSTRAND AVE., BKLYN
718.769.1254
I can always get behind dipping entire roast beef sandwiches in beef juice, and dipping is heartily embraced here. They'll do it for you, or you can have the power with a side of broth.

MY PICKS

Jonathan de Castro

Founder, De Castro Goaltending Academy, Assistant & Goaltending Coach for Manhattanville College, NCAA D III

EAT
WHIT'S END
16702 ROCKAWAY BEACH BLVD., ROCKAWAY
516.746.2205

SHOUT OUT
JAE NYC EATS
JAENYCEATS.COM
My wife's Rockaway Beach–based dessert company.

BEER LEAGUE PICK
MIKHAIL BORTNIK*

EAT
NETCOST MARKET
2339 65TH ST., BKLYN
718.627.7449

I love exotic food, and this is just a haven of it way south in Brooklyn. Loads of packaged goods you've probably never seen and a really large prepared-food section with tastes from across all of the former USSR's different cuisines. Be warned that the staff (and the shoppers) are not friendly and probably will try to speak to you in Russian.*

HONORARY BEER LEAGUER

EAT
BRANDS DELI
44 WEST PARK AVE., LONG BEACH, NY • 516.431.1795

Not technically New York City, but how could we pass up a sandwich shop whose items are named after legends from the hockey world? All categories are included, from locals (The Messiah, Leetchie, King Henrik) to goons (Albanian Assassin, Grim Reaper, The Hammer), with each Original Six team getting their own breakfast sandwich. During the summer, they'll deliver right to the beach, a few blocks south, but more importantly, you can call your order in from a few blocks north, after skating at the Long Beach Municipal Ice Arena.

nyc hub
WESTSIDE SKATE & STICK

174–76 5TH AVE., 5TH FL., NY
212.228.8400

●●●●

Location, location, location. We get it, storefront costs more. Access to foot traffic is a critical factor in consumer retail. So what does it say when the best hockey shop in the largest city in the country is a five-story elevator ride up in an old-school, open-the-door-yourself lift (NB: don't wait for the door to open, or you'll be standing there all day). You'd have to be pretty confident in your clientele, that they'd take a few extra minutes from their lunch hour to bring in their skates for a sharpen and then spread the word, which they do. You'll hear the name "Westside" mentioned in every locker room in the city. The place itself is small and packed, mimicking the same tension you feel at some rinks—the collision of two very disparate worlds, figure skating and hockey. And be warned—you'll probably be late getting back to the office if you happen to ask an innocent question about skate sharpening of owner David Healy or any of his crew. Apparently it's as much of a science as it is a craft, so pull up a chair and take out a notebook.

EAT
EISENBERG'S
SANDWICH SHOP
174 5TH AVE., NY
212.675.5096

As soon as you enter, a waft of NYC circa 1974 washes over you, a smell unique to pre-grade-rated establishments, a metallic merging of meat and grill, which begs the question: Is all the research really in on high-fat diets? We remain, as always, skeptical.

GEAR
PARAGON SPORTS
867 BROADWAY, NY • 212.255.8889

Not the biggest hockey department, but frankly any equipment in the city is a plus. The range of what Paragon does carry is impressive (gear for pretty much every sport), and after Labor Day, they open up a pop-up around the corner for their annual Warehouse Sale, with goods going for 50 to 80 percent off retail. A bit of a madhouse, but if you're early enough, you'll score some cheap mitts and have no problem getting some time and space from the rest of the shoppers.

DRINK
UNION SQUARE GREENMARKET
E. 17TH ST & UNION SQUARE W., NY
212.788.7476

Usual suspects populate the Union Square Greenmarket, and while we're all for grass-fed this and non-GMO that, the "farm to bottle" Orange County Distillery booth caught our eye. With a 1600-square-foot barn in upstate Goshen, NY, holding pretty much their entire operation (vodka, bourbon, rye, single malt, gin), this brand proves the point that the beauty of a farmers market isn't what you aim for but what you stumble upon.

BEER LEAGUE PICK
MELODY TRAN

PING PONG
SPIN NYC
48 E. 23RD ST., NY
212.982.8802

Sometimes, I like to come here on a tournament night just to watch people play ping-pong. I could never get to their level, I'm still chasing the balls 75 percent of the time.

DRINK
PLUG UGLIES
256 3RD AVE., NY
212.780.1944

A sports bar with taste, featuring wine on tap (?), craft cocktails, and shuffleboard. Sneak around the corner and grab a peak at Gramercy Park, a private, gated greenspace open only to residents of the bordering streets, who in the 19th century were issued keys made of gold. Not to worry, the park is open to the public for *one hour* every year, on December 24th. As the guardian of the park says, "It is visibly accessible" to everyone else the rest of the year.

DRINK
TRIONAS ON THIRD
192 3RD AVE., NY • 646.448.4671

NYC has constant beef with Boston, Philly, and LA but basically ignores Chicago, which makes sense, given the success of the Blackhawks (+ Cubs) over the last few years. Serious Irish bar for all Second City fans.

BUY
STRAND BOOKS
828 BROADWAY, NY
212.473.1452

DRINK
OLD TOWN BAR
45 E. 18TH ST., NY • 212.529.6732

Keep it simple: Sit at the bar, order a beer, a burger, and some wings. Give it a minute, and drink in all the details from another century, and I don't mean the last one. From the cash register to the light fixtures (not to mention the bathroom), your time travelling will only enhance your buzz.

While this place might have "18 miles of books" and their sports section can respectfully be called "curated," their hockey selection staggers in at about a foot. But as your blades are being sharpened at Westside, step inside this iconic maze and prove that skaters aren't the thick-necked, monosyllabic bros of days past, but rather inquisitive, voracious readers and citizens of the world. Plus, you'll find a nice array of hats, T-shirts, and messenger bags.

SLEEP / EAT
ACE HOTEL
NEW YORK
20 W. 29TH ST., NY
212.679.2222

They charge you for a bed
and a shower, but what
you're paying for is the
scene. Talk about hubs,
this spot not only trans-
formed an entire neigh-
borhood upon its arrival in
2009 but also immediately
became the go-to lobby
to plug in and meet up.
Grab a lamb burger at the
Breslin, an espresso from
Stumptown, or wait your
turn for a prime co-work-
ing couch.

nyc hub
BROOKLYN BRIDGE PARK

BROOKLYN BRIDGE PARK, PIER 2
718.222.9939

●●●●●●

While the addition of Barclays Center and its accompanying teams (team?) helped upgrade Brooklyn to actual city status, it could be argued that the development of Brooklyn Bridge Park has had an even more profound impact on the borough's identity. Tucked at the end of one of the piers—within this sprawling complex of sports facilities and various eco-friendly diversions—sits a covered roller rink, with easily the most spectacular views from any hockey venue in the city (or any city). Opened in 2014, Pier 2 hosts two roller leagues, but as with most city rinks, it's a challenge getting there, with no car access and the nearest subway a 20-minute walk.

1

2

3

4

HANG
THE PIERS (1)

From simple tables to rolling hills, the piers provide a wide array of choices to sit and stare mindlessly at the downtown skyline. One especially nice touch: Hibachi-style grills ready for your charcoal and meats at Pier 5.

TRANSPORT
SOUTH BROOKLYN FERRY (2)

Runs from Bay Ridge to Wall Street. with stops throughout the South Brooklyn waterfront. Other ferries go other places. Look it up: ferry.nyc

ICE CREAM
BROOKLYN ICE CREAM FACTORY (3)
1 WATER ST., BKLYN
718.246.3963

Located in a converted fireboat house, serves some of the best ice cream in NYC. Be patient; warm weather leads to long lines.

EAT
EMPIRE STORES (4)
53-83 WATER ST., BKLYN
718.858.8555

Massive 19th-century warehouse complex, renovated to include office space and retail outlets such as West Elm and Shinola. Also housed here is the new DUMBO location of the Brooklyn Historical Society.

SURF
AEGIR BOARDWORKS
99 WATER ST., BKLYN
347.987.3825

Dragging your surfboard to DUMBO won't be easy, but if you need some dings repaired, this is your only option in the city. Surf in the summer, skate/snowboard in the winter, with posted hours of operation: 11ish–8ish.

STUFF
MODERN ANTHOLOGY
68 JAY ST., BKLYN
SECOND LOCATION:
123 SMITH ST., BKLYN
718.522.3020

Vintage and vintage-inspired clothing and accessories—what they refer to as "masculine lifestyle," but we call upscale man-cave. As you peruse the merch, you realize you're going in circles, because whether or not you buy anything, you don't really want to leave. The array and quality of what they carry, brands like Saint Rita eyewear and Moore & Giles leather goods, plead with you to invest in your personal grotto. Will you ever use the $265 Bone Pocket Knife from Poglea & Co.? Probably not, but the currency it will emit as it sits on your shelf will make the purchase far more valuable to you than its simple utility.

BEER LEAGUE PICK
BRIAN CURTIN

STUFF
FRONT GENERAL STORE
143 FRONT ST., BKLYN • 646.573.0123

If you lost your luggage on the way to NYC, start here to rebuild your collection. Jeans, belts, shirts, wallets, glasses, jackets, bags, hats, and all sorts of cool stuff you didn't know you wanted. Lots of vintage stylings for men and women, plus all sorts of things for your home or office.

nyc hub
CITY ICE PAVILION

47–32 32ND PLACE, LIC
718.706.6667

On your approach to the rink, whether on foot (about a five-minute walk from the Rawson Street stop on the 7) or by car, you may think you've made a wrong turn, once again losing faith in your GPS. But then you look up and see the bubble on top of what is otherwise a nondescript building on a light-industrial block of Long Island City. Home to the New York City Skyliners (Mite through Midget), the elevator ride from the locker rooms up to the rink is unique to NYC, as is powering through the revolving door at the rink's entrance, all while in full gear. The fun continues after your ice time, on the ride down in the crammed elevator, inches away from the dude you elbowed five minutes earlier.

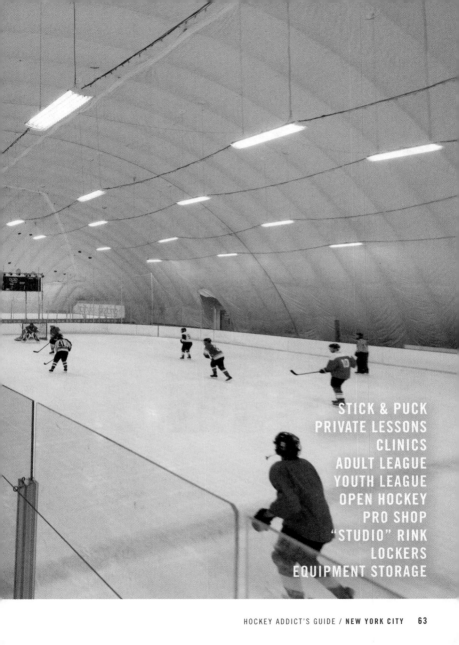

STICK & PUCK
PRIVATE LESSONS
CLINICS
ADULT LEAGUE
YOUTH LEAGUE
OPEN HOCKEY
PRO SHOP
"STUDIO" RINK
LOCKERS
EQUIPMENT STORAGE

SLEEP
THE WILLIAM VALE
111 N. 12TH ST., BKLYN
718.631.8400

Before Murder Inc. Records, there was just plain old Murder Inc., an enforcement "division" of the organized crime families founded by notorious crime figure Benny "Bugsy" Siegel, a Williamsburg native who might squirm in his grave if he could see what has happened to his beloved neighborhood, given his long struggle to establish Las Vegas as the glittering strip of wealth and hope in the desert sands. Jutting towers are on the rise here, one of the newest being this hotel, which has its own 15,000-square-foot elevated park, pool, and requisite rooftop bar / scene, along with balconied rooms and extensive cultural programming. Nice, Bugsy might say, but where's the slots?

BEER
LEAGUE
PICK
MIKHAIL BORTNIK*

COMIC BOOKS
DESERT ISLAND
540 METROPOLITAN AVE., BKLYN
718.388.5087
Great comic bookstore focusing mainly on smaller publishing labels and creator-owned projects. Low-run books and zines, prints, and lots of ephemera. They're super-chill and always game to recommend something. (Take their recommendations.)

* HONORARY BEER LEAGUER

SLEEP
WILLIAMSBURG HOTEL
96 WYTHE AVE., BKLYN
718.362.8100

(1)

BOHEMIAN HALL AND BEER GARDEN [1]
2919 24TH AVE., ASTORIA
718.274.4925
Awesome in warm weather to sit outside at the tables, but usually I'm here during early spring watching the hockey playoffs with friends.

JUDY & PUNCH
34–08 30TH AVE., ASTORIA
718.626.3100
I work here, so . . .

WRITTEN & CURATED BY COLIN EARYES

THE QUAYS PUB
4502 30TH AVE., ASTORIA
718.204.8435
(pronounced THE KEYS) is an Irish bar on 30th Avenue with an awesome staff and neighborhood pub feel. They have a great softball team who can usually be seen here celebrating their wins on Sundays.

THE IRISH EXIT
978 2ND AVE., NY • 212.755.8383
Since I am from Pennsylvania, I never miss a game at the #1 Steelers bar in NYC. I work a 15-hour shift every Saturday until 5 a.m. but you will still see me every Sunday at "The Exit" at 1 p.m. for the games.

MOSAIC
25-19 24TH AVE., ASTORIA
718.728.0708
A fun, laid-back lounge with a large craft beer inventory, sandwiches, and comfy couches and chairs to relax on.

ONE MILE HOUSE
10 DELANCEY ST., NY
646.559.0702
This place has a huge draft list of craft beer that is continually changing, and great cocktails and food too. However, I'm a sucker for burgers, and they do Shame Burger Sundays where a different, oversized, and themed burger is created each weekend!

SLEEP
URBAN COWBOY
111 POWERS ST., BKLYN
347.840.0525

The hockey career of Lyon Porter, owner of Urban Cowboy, spanned nine years and eight leagues, finishing up with the Richmond Riverdogs of the United Hockey League. After he retired, Porter moved on to the real estate business, opening his townhouse-turned-rustic-cabin B&B in 2014. Nestled on a quasi-tree-lined block on the calmer side of Williamsburg, the inn (which he built along with partner Jersey Banks) aims to create a community for like-minded travelers. This boutique dude ranch gives you free reign over the backyard BBQ, a valid record collection, and a roomful of intimates, your fellow guests.

BEER LEAGUE PICK
JASON FAUSTINO

VINYL
ROUGH TRADE
96 WYTHE AVE., BKLYN
718.362.8100
Really strong vinyl collection, and they do a lot for the musicians—showcasing them with live performances and record signings.

CULTURE
MOMA PS1
22–25 JACKSON AVE., LIC
718.784.2084

Originally conceived as a location for site-specific exhibits not available in traditional museums, this quirky outpost of the Museum of Modern Art is now an outer borough institution, five subway stops from Grand Central, all housed in a refurbished public school building.

BARBER
OTIS & FINN
(PICTURED) 111 44TH RD, LIC • 718.433.1155
SECOND LOCATION: 45-22 PEARSON ST., LIC
718.392.2327

Who knew Southern hospitality included a shot of bourbon before a haircut? Two locations, both small, hip, and located in Long Island City. Book online or take your chances walking in.

DRINK
DUTCH KILLS
27–24 JACKSON AVE., LIC
718.383.2724

A true speakeasy—hard to find, dimly intimate, serving potent mixes. You will absolutely miss this spot if you don't look up and catch the blinking "Bar" sign (we paced the block for a while and finally asked a local). Not cheap, but you'll likely appreciate the Prohibition vibe—people tend to value what demands effort. Space is a premium, both at the bar and in the booths. Two tips: Get the jerky and don't steal the metal straws (for sale at the bar).

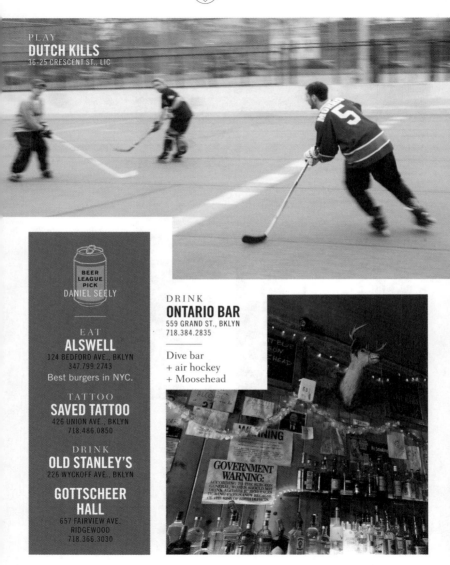

PLAY
DUTCH KILLS
36-25 CRESCENT ST., LIC

BEER LEAGUE PICK
DANIEL SEELY

EAT
ALSWELL
124 BEDFORD AVE., BKLYN
347.799.2743
Best burgers in NYC.

TATTOO
SAVED TATTOO
426 UNION AVE., BKLYN
718.486.0850

DRINK
OLD STANLEY'S
226 WYCKOFF AVE., BKLYN

GOTTSCHEER HALL
657 FAIRVIEW AVE.
RIDGEWOOD
718.366.3030

DRINK
ONTARIO BAR
559 GRAND ST., BKLYN
718.384.2835

Dive bar
+ air hockey
+ Moosehead

THE GUTTER [1]
200 N. 14TH ST., BKLYN
718.387.3585

The back room of a bowling alley in north Williamsburg—it's a perfect divey venue that can handle a decent crowd.

OUR WICKED LADY
153 MORGAN AVE., BKLYN

A cool spot on Morgan Avenue in east Williamsburg that may be the only place that runs rooftop shows.

SUNNYVALE
1031 GRAND ST., BKLYN
347.987.3971

A great venue that's letting us do our album release show there.

GOLD SOUNDS
44 WILSON AVE., BKLYN
718.618.0686

A nice stage with good sound and a room that fills up quick, and is in walking distance from my place.

THE BOWERY ELECTRIC
327 BOWERY, NY
212.228.0228

A midsize club, with a good clear sound system. It's a blast to play here, and they seem to book a lot of great bands from old punk scenes.

WRITTEN &
CURATED BY
MIKE
DUDOLEVITCH

nyc hub
THE SPORT GALLERY

23 8TH AVE., NY
917.262.0753

●●●●

In print for over 50 years, the monthly *SPORT Magazine* was the first to capture the magic of sports in large full-color imagery, with editorial focused not on the scores but on the stories and the aesthetic. Its run ended in 2000, but the brand was brought to new life when former sports writer Wayne Parrish was hired by Post Media (which owned the magazine's photo archives) to open a gallery space to feature the images from the magazine's collection in Toronto's Distillery District. This project eventually led to a bigger idea: An apparel and accessory business, with brands designing products directly inspired by the images—pretty much anything you could throw a logo and colorway onto. With locations in Toronto and Vancouver (where the mag's archives are housed), the NYC outlet of the SPORT Gallery is a small but potent presence in the West Village, a neighborhood not usually known for its sports vibe.

1926

EAT & DRINK
WARREN77
77 WARREN ST., NY
212.227.8994

Opened in 2009 by ex-Ranger Sean Avery, folks flock to this Tribeca hole-in-the-wall still hoping to catch a glimpse of the angry young winger, but having left the biz in 2013, chances of an Avery sighting are slim. On most nights, the place is packed early with hedge-fund suits, but they eventually clear out, leaving a nice hockey-themed environment for catching a game, unless you are a hedge-fund suit, in which case you've probably already cleared out to sit behind the glass at MSG. Also, look out for their occasional bubble hockey tournament.

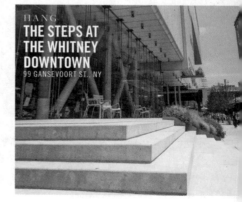

HANG
THE STEPS AT THE WHITNEY DOWNTOWN
99 GANSEVOORT ST., NY

SLEEP
THE STANDARD HIGH LINE
848 WASHINGTON ST., NY
212.645.4646

This one is simple: There's only one hotel to stay at in NYC, and that's the Standard High Line. Why? For no discernable reason, the Standard constructs a beautifully awkward little rink in its front yard every winter, and for a few years even hosted a "What The Puck?!" pond hockey tournament (inset).

PLAY
6TH AVE. &
W. HOUSTON ST.

Flat and relatively smooth, this centrally located asphalt playground makes a good post-work spot for a skate—and since 2010 the site for Jonathan Cohen's annual Rollerhockey Tournament Fundraiser to benefit Ice Hockey in Harlem. The organization's mission, in addition to sponsoring other social and academic programs, is to get kids on the ice who wouldn't ordinarily have the chance.

Bruce Bennett
GETTY IMAGES
DIRECTOR OF
PHOTOGRAPHY,
HOCKEY IMAGERY

"You want to be in the deep corner position, where the goal line intersects with the boards," advises Bruce Bennett, hockey shooter extraordinaire. "You can see the entire ice and, being at ice level, you can see their eyes."

Their eyes. Take for instance Bennett's shot of NJ Devil's Scott Stevens. Initially you might assume it's a faceoff, until you glimpse a distant Penguin (Lemeiux?) in the left distance. So what is Stevens doing, or about to do? An entire arena reduced to a single pair of eyes. A hundred cameras could be parked in that corner, but only Bennett gets that shot, along with other classics: the Nystrom leap, Lanny hugging the Cup, a teenage Gretzky in the locker room.

He's had a camera in his hands since he took his father's Brownie Instamatic on school field trips from his Levittown, Long Island home, wasting countless rolls of film at the Museum of Natural History or the Hayden Planetarium. A bit more serious in college, he headed to Nassau Coliseum to shoot warm-ups of the recently formed NY Islanders, and being new to shooting live sports, the bar was relatively low. "Even if it was out of focus, you were happy to have the image." Happy enough that he sent a few prints to the Montreal-based *Hockey News*. By the following year, he had a press pass and was earning $3 a shot ("negotiated down from $4").

Gamedays, he'd bring a small bag, a camera body, a 135mm lens, and three rolls of film, one for each period, but he was pretty much on his own. "The old-timers wouldn't talk to the young kids; most were secretive about what they were doing."

Eventually, he figured it out (Stanley Cups, Olympics, etc.), mostly by staying focused on hockey. "I shoot very little of anything else. Some scenic photos for fun," he says, though he admittedly likes to look at other kinds of photography for new ideas. "There's always something to pick up from someone else's work. You learn a different way of seeing what you've seen before."

BENNETT'S PICKS

CHEAP
STATEN ISLAND FERRY
Cheapest cruise in town (free).

DRINK
FRAUNCES TAVERN (1)
54 PEARL ST., NY • 212.425.1778
Open since 1762. I was one
of the first diners there. An
institution, mostly for
drinkers.

EAT
THE MARSHAL
628 10TH AVE., NY
212.582.6300
Small restaurant with great
food. So many choices on
10th Avenue.

EAT
BATTERY GARDENS (2)
1 BATTERY PL., NY
212.809.5508
Sunset . . . great view in good
weather.

BEYOND THE HUB

VIRGIL'S REAL BBQ
152 W. 44TH ST., NY • 212.921.9494
The only spot for barbeque in
NYC. Theater crowds will make
the waitstaff try to push you to
give up your table. Order appe-
tizers first, and when you're
done with that, order dinner.

COOKIE DO NYC
550 LAGUARDIA PL., NY
646.892.3600
The newest, hottest place.
Wait on line, it's worth it.

SERENDIPITY3
225 E. 60TH ST., NY • 212.838.3531
Trendy locale. Frozen Hot
Chocolate, nothing like it.
While there, take a two-minute
walk to the tram to Roosevelt
Island. Breathtaking views of
NYC and the UN.

SKATE

THE RINK AT BROOKFIELD PLACE

3 WORLD
FINANCIAL CENTER,
230 VESEY ST., NY
347.843.9503

With the Statue of Liberty on one side and the Freedom Tower on the other, this petite rink's location offers a unique break in the usual sight-seeing itinerary. Open November through March, the ice can get crowded quickly so the earlier in the day the better.

EAT / DRINK
WHITE HORSE TAVERN
567 HUDSON ST., NY
212.989.3956

West Village landmark, their pints of Guiness a rite of passage for all writers, actors, and hangers-on who show up on the city's shores to chase their dreams, celebrate their triumphs and wash away their disappointments. Cash only, due to frequently denied credit cards of the bohemian class (okay, that's a rumor). They also serve a decent burger.

HANG
SEE HAMILTON FOR FREE
75 BROADWAY, NY

Last time we checked, tickets to the theatrical phenomenon were going for about $500 at a minimum, so our suggestion is to take a stroll downtown and check in with the man himself, free of charge, at the Trinity Church Cemetery.

BEER
LEAGUE
PICK
DANIEL SEELY

VINYL
GENERATION RECORDS
210 THOMPSON ST., NY
212.254.1100
The only record store that has ever mattered to me in NYC.

EAT / DRINK
TINY'S AND THE BAR UPSTAIRS
135 WEST BROADWAY, NY
212.374.1135

Does he sit deep in his net? Yeah, but when you're named one of *People* magazine's "World's 100 Most Beautiful People," you get a pass. Does he play half the game looking for his stick? Occasionally, but the fact that Henrik Lundqvist can open a restaurant/bar (see above), have a fashion line, crank out a Slash-like rendition of "Sweet Child O' Mine" on Fallon and *not* be a tool may be his greatest accomplishment, even if he winds up being the Blueshirt version of P. Ewing. Style is about consistency, in and out of the net, and this dude has embraced the city and it has reciprocated. Wait until they raise his number, you'll never see a better flow, both his hair and the tears.

TRIBUTE
9/11 MEMORIAL
180 GREENWICH ST., NY

The quietest crowded spot you'll find in the city. Be prepared for the array of raw emotions that will sneak up on you as you contemplate footprints turned into relecting pools.

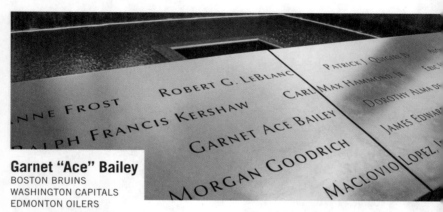

Garnet "Ace" Bailey
BOSTON BRUINS
WASHINGTON CAPITALS
EDMONTON OILERS

Bailey, the Los Angeles Kings' mascot, is a lion, six-foot in stocking feet and wears number 72 (the average temperature in LA, cute). He is the namesake of Garnet "Ace" Bailey, the Kings' director of pro scouting for seven seasons whose time with the team ended the day he boarded United Airlines Flight 175, heading to LA from Boston on September 11, 2001. On the flight as well was amateur scout Mark Bavis. Minnesota Wild coach Bruce Boudreau—then head coach of the Kings' affiliate Manchester (New Hampshire) Monarchs in their inaugural season—was also supposed to be on the flight but had left a day earlier. Ace Bailey's story is a long and winding road in the hockey world. Years earlier, as a veteran player for the Oilers, he had taken a youngster named Wayne under his wing and showed him the ropes, including, prophetically, helping ease the kid's fear of flying. That kid did pretty well for himself and

when he wound up with the Kings, Ace got a call. Ace's Cup rings wouldn't fit on one hand: two as a player with the Boston teams of the early '70s and five as a scout with the Oilers. In between, he played for the expansion Capitals, probably the worst team ever, who at the end of a long losing season in 1975 finally won a road game, their only one of the season (they totalled 21 points in all, a brutal 8-67-5). So excited by this win, Ace took a trash can from the locker room and waltzed around the ice in celebration, no doubt confusing the remainder of the 3,933 folks who had shown up for what must have been a dream matchup with the California Golden Seals at the Oakland-Alameda County Coliseum. Bailey maintained a strong connection to kids throughout his life, and in that spirit, the Ace Bailey Children's Foundation was established to focus on the well-being of hospitalized children (acebailey.org).

VINTAGE
STAR STRUCK
47 GREENWICH AVE., NY
212.691.5357

Friendly staff + rock concert tees + the occasional Isles jacket. Dig and ye shall find.

BEER
LEAGUE
PICK
MELODY TRAN

ACTIVITY
FAT CAT
75 CHRISTOPHER ST., NY
212.675.6056

They have ping-pong, shuffleboard, pool, board games, and a background of live musical acts, usually of the jazz variety. It's a great way to experience live jazz in a very casual setting where you can simultaneously hit balls with your friends. Honestly, I can't think of anything better.

MY PICKS: TEA

Adam Sherlip
EXECUTIVE
DIRECTOR,
THE HOCKEY
FOUNDATION

Tea and hockey may seem an odd pair, but for Adam Sherlip, they have intersected on numerous occasions in his life. The Brooklyn native shares a number of his favorite tea places around the city for skaters that are looking for a place to perk up before, or unwind after, a game.

HARNEY & SONS (1)
433 BROOME ST., NY
212.933.4853
I worked at this store when it first opened (and with the company after), and have been a lover of Harney Tea for many years prior and following my time at the shop. With over 200 teas ranging from the very affordable to very expensive, there's something for everyone, whether you're a newbie or tea snob, and all of it can be enjoyed in the tasting room and cafe.

Due to Sherlip's long association with Harney & Sons, much of the equipment donated to his hockey non-profit (hockeyfoundation. org) is stored in their Millerton, NY warehouse (above, right), along with their tea.

T SHOP
247 ELIZABETH ST., NY
646.726.4086
Quirky store in the back of a building with a psychic shop facing the street, providing a selection of quality seasonal and estate teas, mostly from China and Taiwan.

TÉ SHOP
163 W. 10TH ST., NY • 929.335.3168
Taiwan produces some of the finest oolong (semi-oxidized) teas in the world, and this small shop specializes in oolongs of all varieties while also offering private guided tastings to help enhance the experience.

TEA AND SYMPATHY
108 GREENWICH AVE., NY
212.989.9735
If you love English beer and bitter average-quality black tea with milk and sugar, then this place is for you! The British may be synonymous with tea, but English tea service has fallen out of favor for many folks on both sides of the pond. So much so, that tea companies in London are starting to look more like tea companies in New York. As a result, "afternoon tea" has become something nostalgic for Brits and Americans alike; but it's still worth seeking out.

MATCHABAR
256 W. 15TH ST., NY • 212.627.1058
Brooklyn-based company with a location near Chelsea Piers, specializing in matcha: matcha drinks, matcha pastries, matcha anything. You can find their RTD (ready to drink) bottles of matcha at Whole Foods and other grocers/bodegas.

TEA DRUNK
123 E. 7TH ST., NY
917.573.9936
Surprisingly peaceful little shop near Tompkins Square Park that specializes in high-end Chinese tea, and when I say "high-end," I mean one of the teas they sell goes for $399!

CHA-AN TEAHOUSE
230 E. 9TH ST., NY • 212.228.8030
Easy to miss but worth finding, this second-floor haven offers a nice selection of teas from around Asia.

MATCHA CAFE WABI
233 E. 4TH ST., NY
This hole-in-the-wall focuses on Japanese snacks and drinks—namely, matcha. Lovers of this stone-ground green tea flock here for that extra bolt of natural energy that only matcha provides (due to the fact you're ingesting the tea leaves rather than just drinking their "broth").

TEN REN'S TEA AND GINSENG CO.
75 MOTT ST., NY • 212.349.2286
5817 8TH AVE., BKLYN
718.853.0660
135-18 ROOSEVELT AVE., FLUSHING
718.461.9305
Ten Ren is the shop responsible for introducing New Yorkers to high-quality teas from Taiwan and China when it opened on Canal Street in 1984. With over 70 stores in Taiwan, and 3 in NYC, they offer excellent oolongs and greens, as well as an assortment of pu'erh, black tea, and white teas, along with bubble tea to go.

HAMPTON CHUTNEY CO.
143 GRAND ST., NY
212.226.9996
464 AMSTERDAM AVE., NY
212.362.5050
Hampton Chutney Co. not only has some of the most delicious masala chai outside of India, but also has a delicious menu of dosas (Indian crepes).

IPPODO
125 E. 39TH ST., NY • 212.370.0609
Matcha-to-go from Kyoto, Japan based tea specialist, the home of the Japanese tea ceremony (which uses matcha—stone-ground Japanese green tea).

RADIANCE TEA HOUSE & BOOKS
158 W. 55TH ST., NY • 212.217.0442
208 E. 50TH ST., NY • 212.888.8060
Delicious Asian fusion fare with a lovely, albeit slightly expensive, tea selection, in locations that feel like an oasis.

ALICE'S TEA CUP
CHAP. 1: 102 W. 73RD ST., NY
212.799.3006
CHAP. 2: 156 E. 64TH ST., NY
212.486.9200
CHAP. 3: 220 E. 81ST ST., NY
212.734.4832
I'm not gonna lie, I don't love Alice's Tea Cup. It's themed like Alice in Wonderland, it's too cutesy and it's too stuffy. That being said, a lot of mothers love to bring their daughters here for an assortment of tea parties in an English "afternoon tea" setting.

PUERH BROOKLYN
174 GRAND ST., BKLYN
347.510.8136
The name may suggest a menu limited to pu'erh, the only truly fermented tea (kombucha is a fermented product made with tea, and other teas are simply oxidized, not fermented), but this quaint shop has a fine assortment of teas (many organic) and a number of events to inform tea lovers of all levels.

BELLOCQ
104 WEST ST., BKLYN • 800.495.5416
Meticulously curated teas with sophisticated packaging and presentation in a tiny retail space, not far from City Ice.

COMMUNITEALIC
11-11 46TH RD., LIC • 718.729.7708
As much a restaurant/cafe with beer and cider as it is a tea shop.

FANG GOURMET TEA
135-25 ROOSEVELT AVE., FLUSHING
888.888.0216
This list wouldn't be complete without an authentic Chinese tea shop from Flushing, near World Ice. Fang Tea specializes in teas from China: oolong, pu'erh, jasmine greens, top-notch white & black teas, and an assortment of traditional herbs.

nyc hub
NHL STORE
1185 6TH AVE., NY
212.221.6375

Okay, so here's the plan: Since NHL corporate headquarters are right upstairs from the store, grab a Lundqvist jersey or a Tavares doll (or something else), head up on the elevator, and ask for Gary B. at reception. Commandeer a conference room, break out your notes, and then walk him through the changes to the game you've drawn up. And you might want to get a jump on this, since within the next year the NHL, along with the retail location, is planning to pack up and move to new—no doubt shiny—digs in Manhattan's new Hudson Yards district, which is in screaming distance from Madison Square Garden.

SKATE

THE RINK AT ROCKEFELLER CENTER

5TH AVE., BETWEEN
49TH & 50TH ST., NY
212.332.7654

Open October to April, adult rates from $25 to $32 (kids 10 and under $15) and an additional $12 for skate rental. Cost aside, the appeal is strictly bucket-list.

PRO PICK	EAT	SLEEP
Adam McQuaid BOSTON BRUINS	**TAO UPTOWN** 42 E. 58TH ST., NY 212.888.2288	**RITZ-CARLTON** 50 CENTRAL PARK SOUTH, NY 212.308.9100

SLEEP
POD 39 HOTEL
145 E. 39TH ST., NY
844.763.7666

They call their rooms "pods" because they're really small, like *really* small, like 90 square-feet small ("mini bunk" pods). Here's a plan: Grab a few tacos (on premises at Salvation Taco), fight your way to the rooftop bar, throw a few back, and then stumble your way to your "pod" and pack it in, literally. One bunk for you and one for the bag.

SKATE
WOLLMAN RINK IN CENTRAL PARK
CENTRAL PARK BETWEEN
E. 62ND & 63RD ST., NY
212.439.6900

Infamous rink "saved" by you-know-who (clue: curious hair), open late October to early April, has twice-weekly late-night hockey clinics, plus youth clinics and an in-house league. Enter the park at Central Park South (59th Street) and 6th Avenue.

EAT
THE HALAL GUYS
53RD ST. & 6TH AVE., NY

The Halal Guys are the true original and makes the best street food in the city. Do not support the imposters! I recommend the lamb and chicken combo over rice with their famous white sauce, and some BBQ or red (hot) sauce too, if you're feeling spicy. Love it so much I designed an Extra Butter x Reebok "Street Meat" Ventilator Sneaker after it, and you can still find a working Halal truck decked out in our design roaming around the city. If the line is too long on 53rd and 6th (southeast corner), they do have a second cart on the southwest corner. They have an actual restaurant on 14th Street and 1st Avenue, but you're soft if you didn't wait on line and get it on the street.

SKATE
BANK OF AMERICA WINTER VILLAGE AT BRYANT PARK
6TH AVE.,
BETWEEN 40TH & 42ND ST., NY

A big name for a small rink, but it is a treat to stumble upon a sheet surrounded by midtown towers. And though they host an occasional pond tournament, the rink is primarily for skating only (we were even told to remove our hockey gloves). Skating is free, as is a locker, but rentals will run $20 and locks an additional $10. Open late October through early March.

SLEEP
CITIZEN M
218 W. 50TH ST., NY
212.461.3638

Small, efficient, sound-proof rooms all controlled by a MoodPad tablet, from the TV to window blinds to wake-up acoustics. Self check-in, along with a unique common space and rooftop bar, accompanied by a wink-and-nod visual aesthetic.

CAFFEINE
FIKA BRYANT PARK
114 W. 41ST ST., NY
212.840.0677

"No pictures," they told us, even though we said we were making a guidebook for hockey players, and despite the fact that this chain is Swedish and Sweden has a very rich hockey heritage, recently winning the World Championship, plus there's Henrik Lundqvist, Jesper Fast, Ulf Samuelsson, Ulf Nillson . . . "No pictures." Anyway, great coffee.

HANG
NY PUBLIC LIBRARY STEPS
476 5TH AVE.

PRO PICK

Kevan Miller
BOSTON BRUINS

EAT / DRINK
NOBU FIFTY-SEVEN
40 W. 57TH ST., NY
212.757.3000

PRO SHOP
YOUTH HOUSE LEAGUE
YOUTH TRAVEL
ADULT LEAGUE
ADULT DEVELOPMENTAL LEAGUE
OPEN HOCKEY
TRAINING CENTER
PRIVATE INSTRUCTION
EQUIPMENT STORAGE
FOOD COURT

nyc hub
SKY RINK AT CHELSEA PIERS

PIER 61, CHELSEA PIERS
212.336.6100

●●●●●

Like the pre-Wi-Fi subway, the ice has always been a place where the world can't reach you, a frozen oasis away from the daily grind. Anyone who has ever laced them up recognizes this priceless benefit, and nowhere is this more evidenced than at Chelsea Piers. Without naming names, these rinks are home to renowned actors, artists, ex-NHL'ers (even an occasional politician on "hiatus"), all who come to have a good skate . . . and be left alone. Should you come across one of these folks at a midday open or late-night league game, please give them a break and, if you must make conversation, restrict your banter to ice matters. The rink itself: Originally located on the top floor of a midtown office building (hence the name "Sky Rink"), Chelsea Piers is the only location in Manhattan to skate year-round and is home to the NY Cyclones (Tier II/AA, Mite through Midget), the New York City Gay Hockey Association, and a robust Adult Development program.

THE HIGH LINE

This stretch of out-of-service railroad track (an eyesore ignored for decades) was reimagined in 1999 as a public space by Chelsea residents Joshua David and Robert Hammond. The first section opened in 2009, with the last completed in 2017 as part of the Hudson Yards Project. A similar project, QueensWay, has been proposed for an abandoned section of the Rockaway Beach Branch of the Long Island Railroad in Queens.

DRINK
THE HALF KING
505 W. 23RD ST., NY • 212.462.4300

Co-founded by writer / filmmaker Sebastian Junger (*The Perfect Storm*, *Restrepo*) as a hangout for journalists, this solid pub is known more for its monthly reading series than for its menu options. Game night, you might have to snag the remote to switch away from CNN to find the match.

PRO PICK	SLEEP
Kevan Miller	**HOTEL GANSEVOORT**
BOSTON BRUINS	18 9TH AVE., NY
	212.206.6700

BUY
STORY
144 10TH AVE., NY
212.242.4853

A permanent pop-up, with rotating products inspired by a temporary narrative theme (disruption, wellness, etc.). Great spot to find that (usually expensive) gift for the person that has everything.

SID'S BIKES [1]
151 W. 19TH ST., NY • 212.989.1060
Huge bike shop. Mostly a high-end road bike outfitter, but they sell tires and tubes for good prices and have helpful mechanics.

BFOLD
224 E. 13TH ST., NY
212.529.7247
This is the place to go if you want a folding bicycle. They sell and repair all the best folding brands.

RED LANTERN BICYCLES
345 MYRTLE AVE., BKLYN
347.889.5338
My favorite shop in New York. There's a cafe in the front serving a great vegan sandwich, coffee, and beer. They have a decent selection of used bikes, do solid repairs in their no-frills shop, and their prices are fair. Make sure to pet the shop cat.

DIXON'S BICYCLE SHOP [2]
792 UNION ST., BKLYN •
718.636.0067
A neighborhood institution in Park Slope. A basic sales and repair shop run by good people.

KING KOG
453 GRAHAM AVE., BKLYN
347.689.2299
King Kog is a full-service repair shop, but this is also where you go to find vintage track frames, road frames, and components, as well as accessories and gear.

WRITTEN &
CURATED BY
BRITON MALCOMSON

CAFFEINE
UNDERLINE COFFEE
511 W. 20TH ST., NY
917.477.9476

Tasteful and cozy,
directly under the
Highline, a small
port in the crazy city
storm. (NB:
no bathrooms)

EAT / DRINK / BUY
CHELSEA MARKET
75 9TH AVE., NY • 212.652.2110

Indoor shopping / eating bazaar offering a
ridiculously diverse range of cuisines to a
predominately touristy crowd. Worth a walk
through, however its lack of windows com-
bined with extreme crowds has been known
to lead to mild panic attacks.

DRINK
SMITHFIELD HALL
138 W. 25TH ST., NY
212.929.9677

Proudly and primarily a footy (soccer)
bar, you'll need to be OK in a room full
of Anglophiles all at "sixes and sevens" as
their team gets a "comprehensive thrashing"
because their "dodgy keeper" lets in another
"pea-roller."

UPRIGHT CITIZENS BRIGADE CHELSEA [1]

307 W. 26TH ST., NY
212.366.9176

If you're planning on seeing improv in the city, this is the place. Asssscat is the hot ticket on Sunday nights—all the best improvisors from UCBs past and present can suddenly turn up and make for a fun show. Monday nights have a free midnight stand-up show called Whiplash that's also a good bet.

WRITTEN &
CURATED BY
JIM LESTER

UCB EAST

153 E. 3RD ST., NY
212.366.9231

The East Village location of the UCB offers more of a mix of stand-up and improv. The big nights are Wednesdays, Fridays and Saturdays. The venue has a beer and wine bar to hang out in, great chance to have a drink with performers.

CREEK & CAVE

10-93 JACKSON AVE., LIC
718.706.8783

It's mostly stand-up now, but it's a really fun space. Best part is it's attached to a solid Cal-Mex restaurant.

COMEDY CELLAR

117 MACDOUGAL ST., NY
212.254.3480

Great little stand-up spot, featured in the opening of *Louie*. Has the feel of a secret underground club, but everyone knows about it.

PEOPLES IMPROV THEATER

123 E. 24TH ST., NY
212.563.7488

A cool place. You enter the venue through the bar, where you can hang out before and after shows. They have a main stage and a basement stage. Good alternative to UCB.

MY PICKS

Chris Cosentino

HEAD COACH, NYU HOCKEY

Hockey game nights at Chelsea Piers are insane, and the atmosphere is electric. We take an incredible amount of pride in being New York City's college hockey team and, like athletes, the NYU coaching staff has a game-day routine. Depending on how the game goes, post-game drink locations will vary, but there are a few options in the West Village and in Chelsea. Also, as a part of New York City's college hockey team, you need to look the part, especially at NYU. Fun fact: NYU Hockey Assistant Coach Mike Martin was featured in a J. Crew hockey shoot.

GAME DAY LUNCH
BOTTINO TO GO
246 10TH AVE., NY
212.206.6766

PREGAME DINNER
THE MEATBALL SHOP
200 9TH AVE., NY
212.257.4363

PREGAME COFFEE
LA BERGAMOTE
177 9TH AVE., NY
212.627.9010

APPAREL
SPECTRE & CO (1)
CHELSEA MARKET
75 9TH AVE., NY
914.589.0982

CURATED BASICS (2)
CHELSEA MARKET
75 9TH AVE., NY

LULULEMON MEATPACKING (3)
408 W. 14TH ST., NY
212.255.2978

nyc hub
BARCLAYS CENTER
620 ATLANTIC AVE., BKLYN • 917.618.6100

How long the Islanders remain in Brooklyn is anyone's guess, so whatever is written here is destined to be outdated by the time it is read; welcome to the limitations of the printed word, book-wise. All sides in this endless saga negotiate through the press, so truth remains, as always, intangible. Wang's Lighthouse Project, Frank Gehry, Bruce Ratner, Jon Ledecky, eminent domain, the land grab, the rumors, the money . . . irrelevant, because all we want—all we ever wanted—is the NHL in BK. Will they move to a new arena in Queens (Willets Point), or to Kansas City or Seattle or Quebec or back to Nassau County (Belmont) or simply to a refurbished, de-obstructed Brooklyn? Will Jay Z step in and settle it? The building itself, visually arresting and immediately iconic, is a true statement, but why didn't they take rink size into account when it was designed? However odd the answer may turn out to be, it's sure to fit nicely into the long, strange trip that the Isles franchise has taken—from 1972 until today, whenever that is.

EAT / DRINK
BERG'N
899 BERGEN ST., BKLYN • 718.857.2337

The founders of Brooklyn Flea and Smorgasburg are behind this indoor beer garden (plus some outside seating), with food-truck-style offerings at one end (Mighty Quinn's, Lumpia Shack) and a coffee bar at the other. In the middle sit large, shared tables and a big screen to watch whatever. You might trip over a few strollers (or toddlers for that matter), but the cement floor keeps the sound level high, so no one will hear you apologize.

BEER LEAGUE PICK
BRIAN CURTIN

EAT
MILE END DELI
97A HOYT ST., BKLYN
718.852.7510
SECOND LOCATION:
53 BOND ST., NY • 212.529.2990

Smoked meat poutine and Labatt Blue, what more do you need to know about this ode to Montreal? One intriguing option—the Ruth Wilensky sandwich, which costs extra to order sans mustard. Even the bathroom is Canadiens-themed with vintage Habs pictures.

STUFF
PARK DELICATESSAN
722 CLASSON AVE., BKLYN • 718.789.8889

Why is it called a delicatessan? "Because there was a deli here and we kept the display cases," says owner Michael Sclafani. Why flowers? "They're cool." Why skateboards? "Because flowers with skateboards are cooler than just flowers." In addition to the retail location, Sclafani & Co. have their own Park Deli brand of apparel, available in the Brooklyn Museum gift shop, and at the occasional Tokyo pop-up.

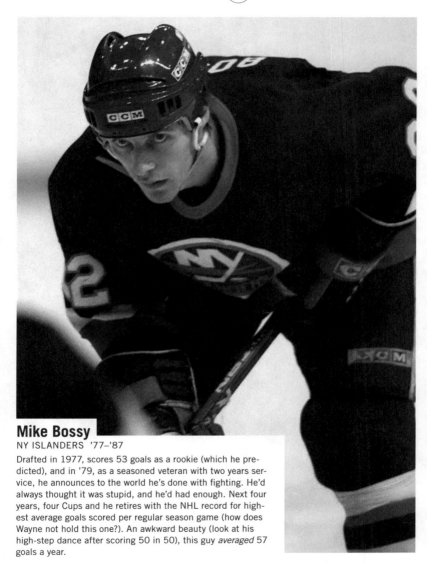
Mike Bossy
NY ISLANDERS '77–'87

Drafted in 1977, scores 53 goals as a rookie (which he predicted), and in '79, as a seasoned veteran with two years service, he announces to the world he's done with fighting. He'd always thought it was stupid, and he'd had enough. Next four years, four Cups and he retires with the NHL record for highest average goals scored per regular season game (how does Wayne not hold this one?). An awkward beauty (look at his high-step dance after scoring 50 in 50), this guy *averaged* 57 goals a year.

John Tavares
NY ISLANDERS
'09–PRESENT

Barclays Center produced its first iconic hockey moment when John Tavares scored in double overtime to eliminate the Florida Panthers and move on to the second round of the 2016 playoffs, ending a 23-year, playoff-series-winning drought. Four Panthers were below the hashmarks, in addition to a bewildered Luongo in net, as the quietest superstar willed a wraparound into a gaping net. Thanks for the memory.

DRINK
THE ADIRONDACK
1241 PROSPECT AVE., BKLYN
718.871.0100

We had just gotten off the ice at Lakeside and were figuring out where to drink. One of the skaters, Brandon, suggested we go to his bar. His bar? Not sure what he meant (owned or frequented?), we went. Turns out he owns it. Nothing tastes better than cold beer after being on the ice, or so we thought. Truth: Nothing tastes better than *free* cold beer after being on the ice. Specializing in New York State breweries, it's right on the F/G. Not by, on.

STUFF
BROOKLYN DRONES NYC
315 4TH AVE., BKLYN • 929.337.6414

Be honest: If you don't already own one, you definitely want one, and you're not even sure why. This spot ("a store for all your aerial photo and video needs") has you covered. They offer drones for sale, repair service, and classes to learn how to operate them. One spot to legally fly a drone in Brooklyn without a permit: Calvert Vaux Park in Gravesend.

PLAY
LEFRAK AT LAKESIDE
PROSPECT PARK, NEAR OCEAN AVE.
AND LINCOLN RD. ENTRANCE

Granted, Lefrak is an architectural wonder. You barely see it until it's in front of you, which is no small feat for two large rinks in the middle of a park. Upon completion, however, a few details were missed, such as benches (what??), a remedy for which we're told is in the works. We hope so, since changing lines by opening the door to the rink leads to some challenging situations. Two sheets, both outdoors, one designed for hockey and covered, the other for general skating under the stars. Ice in the fall and winter, roller in the spring and summer.

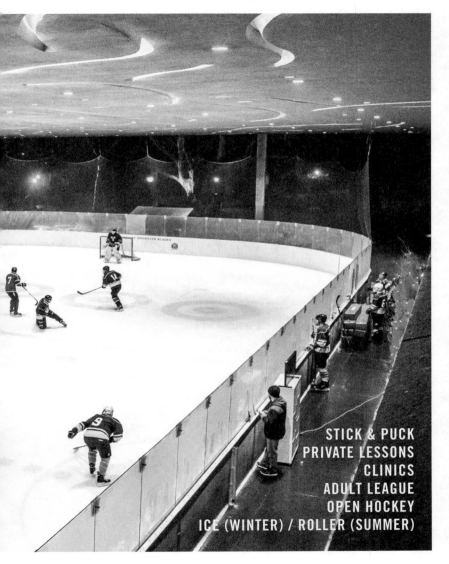

STICK & PUCK
PRIVATE LESSONS
CLINICS
ADULT LEAGUE
OPEN HOCKEY
ICE (WINTER) / ROLLER (SUMMER)

MY PICKS

Alyse Barker

NY ISLANDERS,
IN-ARENA HOST

Watching the pros fly across the ice is what sells the beer, but intermission at Barclays brings another spectacle: Alyse Barker making her way across the frozen surface . . . in heels. "Everyone freaks out about it," she says. "It's pretty easy, I just glide vs. step." After being crowned Miss New York and becoming a member of the New York Jets Flight Crew Cheerleaders, 2017–2018 marks her third season pumping up the crowd for New York Islanders' home games. "Growing up, hockey was always on in my house," says Barker. "Now, it's an incredible feeling to be a part of a great organization."

EAT
AGAVE
140 7TH AVE S., NY • 212.989.2100
I love any place that does a bottomless brunch.

KORZO (1)
667 5TH AVE., BKLYN • 718.499.1199
As a first generation Slovak American, I'm excited to go to this place.

THE CROOKED KNIFE
29 E. 30TH ST., NY • 212.696.2593

SPA
ROMEO & JULIETTE LASER
5 E. 57TH ST., NY • 212.750.2000

GYM
NYSC LAB: STOKED 360
with Kira Stokes
555 6TH AVE., NY • 917.382.5573

HAIR SALON
THREE SQUARES STUDIO
444 W. 17TH ST., NY
917.847.3384
Lynette Hernden and Paul Pesce keep me looking game day ready and my best.

MUSIC
BEACON THEATRE
2124 BROADWAY, NY
212.465.6500

THE BITTER END
147 BLEECKER ST., NY
212.673.7030

COMEDY
NY COMEDY CLUB
241 E. 24TH ST., NY • 212.696.5233

DENTIST
GOODMAN ORTHODONTICS
440 E. 57TH ST., APT. 1A, NY
212.688.4663
Dr. Adam Goodman makes sure my smile is perfect for game day! He's also a big Isles fan!

HANG
CENTRAL PARK
The Great Lawn, of course. I bring my pup and go to the dog-friendly area.

DAY TRIPS
LONG BEACH, NY
Just a quick ride on the LIRR, and my toes are in the sand.

LONG BEACH ISLAND, NJ
Another go-to spot for me.

BEER
LEAGUE
PICK
MELODY TRAN

ACTIVITY
ROYAL PALMS SHUFFLEBOARD CLUB
514 UNION ST., BKLYN
347.223.4410

For a lot of my life, I thought shuffleboard was a table game that involved sand because that's the only version I ever saw of it. But then, I went to the Royal Palms Shuffleboard Club and was completely blown away. It's REAL shuffleboard!! The bar theme is cruise ship/cabana, and the vibe definitely feels like you're on vacation. The drinks are amazing, and there are board games to play while you wait, including life-sized Jenga!

Denis Potvin

NY ISLANDERS '73–'88

Madison Square Garden, mid-season 1979, Rangers Swedish import Ulf Nilsson takes a high hit from Denis Potvin and breaks an ankle. Was the hit cheap? No, certainly not by late '70s standards. (It's possible his ankle would not have broken had his skate not gotten caught in a rut.) Did Nilsson's absence hinder the team? They beat the Isles in the playoffs that year. Nonetheless, for the remainder of that game,

whenever Potvin touched the puck, the crowd let loose with "POTVIN SUCKS!" Added later was a series of strange, singsong whistles, repeated exactly three times, and then punctuated by three resonant syllables . . . "Pot-vin-sucks." The birth of the chant occurred prior to the Isles' dynastic run, but its longevity can be ascribed to one fact: as the years have passed, the Rangers' faithful have maintained a healthy grudge over the four consecutive

Cups that went to the start-ups from the potato fields out East (okay, that's a geographical stretch), captained each time by Potvin, who won the Norris three times before ever touching a Cup. Now engrained in Ranger game-day culture as well as that of MSG itself (you'll probably hear it at a Knicks game), the chant speaks to a deep-seated pain, that will endure at least until the Blueshirts cobble together a dynasty of their own.

EAT
JALAPA JAR
100 HENRY ST., BKLYN
384 SCHERMERHORN ST., BKLYN
347.689.2654

Salsa and eggs in the subway—we're there. Don't let the address fool you, their original spot is, in fact, underground though a second location recently popped up around the corner from Barclays.

DRINK
CAMP
179 SMITH ST., BKLYN
718.852.8086

Now that the adult-summer-camp craze has finally been snuffed out (please say it has), you can still grab a board game and sit in front of a fire in this log-cabin-inspired bar.

EAT
BONNIE'S GRILL
555 5TH AVE., BKLYN • 718.499.7999

A middlebrow greasy spoon featuring a Buffalo-favorite roast beef on weck, a fine burger, and a nice pulled-pork sandwich. The wings are meh, perhaps because the expectation is simply too high. Established by Buffalo native Mike Naber, the venue has changed hands but kept its Queen City spirit.

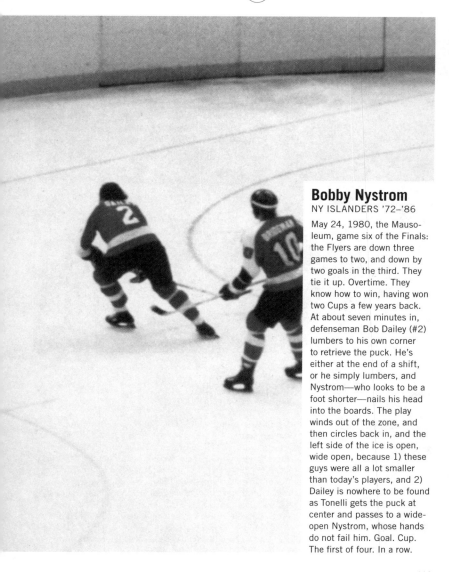
Bobby Nystrom
NY ISLANDERS '72–'86

May 24, 1980, the Mausoleum, game six of the Finals: the Flyers are down three games to two, and down by two goals in the third. They tie it up. Overtime. They know how to win, having won two Cups a few years back. At about seven minutes in, defenseman Bob Dailey (#2) lumbers to his own corner to retrieve the puck. He's either at the end of a shift, or he simply lumbers, and Nystrom—who looks to be a foot shorter—nails his head into the boards. The play winds out of the zone, and then circles back in, and the left side of the ice is open, wide open, because 1) these guys were all a lot smaller than today's players, and 2) Dailey is nowhere to be found as Tonelli gets the puck at center and passes to a wide-open Nystrom, whose hands do not fail him. Goal. Cup. The first of four. In a row.

PLAY
FORT HAMILTON
ROLLER RINK
5200 FT. HAMILTON PKWY., BKLYN
718.435.7342

EAT & DRINK
GREENWOOD PARK
555 7TH AVE., BKLYN • 718.499.7999

Word association: Emile "The Cat" Francis (onetime
Rangers goalie, GM, and coach); "Cat Scratch Fever," Ted
Nugent's late '70s riff-powered classic (wing-nut politics a
typical outgrowth of riff-powered rock). Nugent, as it turns
out, is the birth father of restaurateur Ted Mann, founder
of South Slope's Greenwood Park, a 13,000 square-foot,
indoor-outdoor beer garden, converted from a former gas
station / mechanic shop. Full circle: Francis hails from
North Battleford, Saskatchewan, Canada, also the hometown of Corey Schwab—backup keeper for the 2003 Cup–
winning NJ Devils—whose father was the town's auto
mechanic (okay, the last bit probably isn't true).

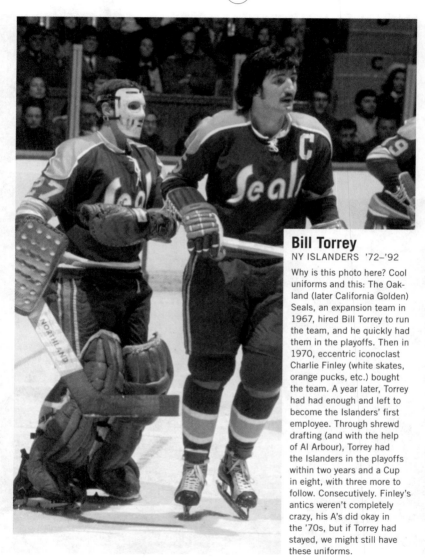
Bill Torrey
NY ISLANDERS '72–'92

Why is this photo here? Cool uniforms and this: The Oakland (later California Golden) Seals, an expansion team in 1967, hired Bill Torrey to run the team, and he quickly had them in the playoffs. Then in 1970, eccentric iconoclast Charlie Finley (white skates, orange pucks, etc.) bought the team. A year later, Torrey had had enough and left to become the Islanders' first employee. Through shrewd drafting (and with the help of Al Arbour), Torrey had the Islanders in the playoffs within two years and a Cup in eight, with three more to follow. Consecutively. Finley's antics weren't completely crazy, his A's did okay in the '70s, but if Torrey had stayed, we might still have these uniforms.

WORLD ICE ARENA

13135 AVERY AVE., FLUSHING
718.760.9001

Few would imagine that some of the best ice in the city could be found in the far reaches of Queens, but sharing a roof with an Olympic-sized pool seems to have benefitted World Ice Arena in Flushing Meadow Park. While the rink no longer has an adult hockey league, it still hosts open skates and open hockey throughout the week.

**PRO SHOP
YOUTH IN-HOUSE
SKATING LESSONS
STICK & PUCK
OPEN HOCKEY**

WRITTEN, CURATED &
PHOTOGRAPHED BY
ANDRE LEGASPI

EAT
XI'AN FAMOUS FOODS
41-10 MAIN ST., Flushing • 212.786.2068

Now a city-wide chain, Xi'an Famous Foods has garnered national attention as one of the authorities on Northern Chinese cuisine. The hand-pulled noodles, swimming in a spicy pool of chili and sesame oils, can be a challenge to eat as you try to reel in the endless ribbons of carby goodness, but they're worth the mess. But be warned—when asked what level of spiciness you'd like, know that "mild" can still have one hell of a kick.

DRINK
ZEBRA LOUNGE
13611 38TH AVE.
FLUSHING
718.886.7366

Karaoke, sports, and booze. Nailing all three lands this Flushing bar a spot in my heart as well as a spot on this list. The dark, semi-private booths feature large flat screen televisions beaming the Rangers or Yankees, depending on the time of year. Once the game's over, and your blood-alcohol level has been optimized, reach for a microphone, which are handed out to anyone wanting to channel their inner diva.

EAT
NAN XIANG XIAO LONG BAO
38-12 PRINCE ST., FLUSHING
718.321.3838

The debate over where the best soup dumplings, or xiaolongbao, are made in New York City is one that might never be settled. But Nan Xiang Xiao Long Bao is always in the running, no matter the critic. Located in the heart of Flushing, this gem can easily be found by looking for the line stretched out around Prince Street. Make sure you hit up an ATM beforehand though since it's cash only for those glorious globules.

DRINK
A+ ROOF LOUNGE
39-16 COLLEGE POINT BLVD.
FLUSHING
718.869.1691

Sitting atop the Parc Hotel, the A+ Roof Lounge is a small bar that provides a unique view with sweeping panoramas of the city. From one corner of the roof, you can take in the entire skyline of Manhattan, peek over the centerfield wall of Citifield, and watch planes land in LaGuardia—all while knocking back a few.

ACTIVITY
FLUSHING MEADOW

In addition to being home to World Ice Arena, this enormous park offers an endless list of things to do and see. For starters, there's Citifield, home of the New York Mets, and the USTA National Tennis Center, home of the US Open. Then you have the Queens Museum, the Queens Zoo, New York Hall of Science, the famed Unisphere, (alongside other vestiges of the 1964 World's Fair), a goddamned Putt-Putt course, and much, much more. Those with an appetite would be wise to visit in the summer when the park becomes home to the Queens Night Market. On these Saturday nights, local restaurants and vendors emerge to celebrate the borough's diversity by cooking up some tasty eats.

PLAY
GEORGE HARVEY PARK

144 WHITESTONE EXPY.
WHITESTONE
212.639.9675

Queens is home to a surprisingly big roller-hockey community, and George Harvey is one of the many asphalt rinks in the borough. While the city hasn't done much to maintain many of the other roller-hockey rinks, George Harvey's surface has luckily aged the best. And thanks to dependable lighting that illuminates nightly pick-up games and a youth league that regularly skates here, it's been a mainstay in northern Queens.

future nyc hub
KINGSBRIDGE NATIONAL ICE CENTER
WEST KINGSBRIDGE RD., THE BRONX

If "go big or go home" sounds familiar, it's probably because rumors circulating over the last few years regarding Mr. Messier's grand project in the only borough attached to mainland America. With the first phase scheduled to be completed in late 2020, the NYC hockey landscape will be forever recalibrated with the arrival of the world's largest indoor ice skating complex—a 750,000-square-foot, multi-level behemouth, calling for nine ice rinks, a 5,000-seat arena, training facilities, a concierge equipment cleaning and storage service, and 450 parking spots. Oh, and it sits on a subway stop. Given that real estate prices in the detached boroughs have escalated beyond comprehension, it's a reasonable guess that anyone who plays hockey will probably be moving to the Bronx in the next few years. #thenextbrooklyn

NORTHWELL HEALTH ICE CENTER
AT EISENHOWER PARK
EAST MEADOW, NY

NYC
Beyond the Hubs

●●●●

STATEN ISLAND
NYPD VS FDNY
NEWARK, NEW JERSEY
LOCAL HISTORY
LOCAL COLOR
TRI-STATE AREA RINKS & PRO SHOPS
DAY TRIPS
BEER LEAGUE LINEUP

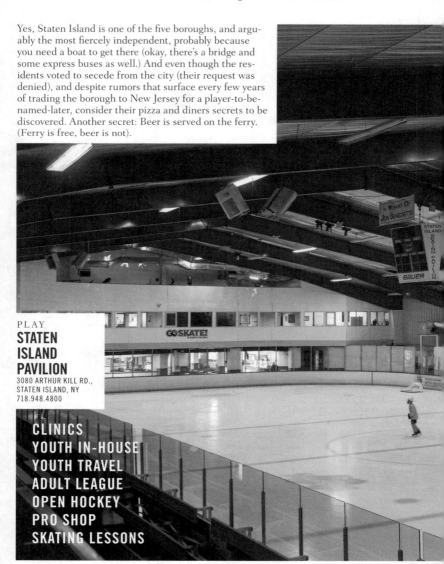

Yes, Staten Island is one of the five boroughs, and arguably the most fiercely independent, probably because you need a boat to get there (okay, there's a bridge and some express buses as well.) And even though the residents voted to secede from the city (their request was denied), and despite rumors that surface every few years of trading the borough to New Jersey for a player-to-be-named-later, consider their pizza and diners secrets to be discovered. Another secret: Beer is served on the ferry. (Ferry is free, beer is not).

PLAY
STATEN ISLAND PAVILION
3080 ARTHUR KILL RD.,
STATEN ISLAND, NY
718.948.4800

CLINICS
YOUTH IN-HOUSE
YOUTH TRAVEL
ADULT LEAGUE
OPEN HOCKEY
PRO SHOP
SKATING LESSONS

Nick Fotiu
NY RANGERS
'76–'79, '80–'85

Only Ranger ever born on Staten Island, Fotiu wound up with the Blueshirts after a few years in the WHA, spending time with the team for two separate runs. Always a favorite of the blue-seat lunch pail set, he's still an active ambassador for the franchise.

PLAY
KB HOCKEY & SKATING FACILITY
1305 C TRAVIS AVE.
STATEN ISLAND, NY
718.682.1350

State-of-the-art ice hockey training and skating center, including a custom-built ice rink, off-ice training room, advanced synthetic and skating treadmill. Hockey lessons are available along with learn-to-skate, goalie clinics, and treadmill lessons.

RIVALRY
FDNY VS NYPD
BARCLAYS CENTER, BKLYN

In a tradition almost half-a-century old, New York's Bravest (the Fire Department) square off every year against New York's Finest (the Police Department). In theory, the game could be referred to as a "friendly," however in practice, this is never the case. No one fights like brothers, right?

NEW JERSEY DEVILS
PRUDENTIAL CENTER
25 LAFAYETTE ST., NEWARK, NJ

Never listed among the top NHL barns, along with Montreal's Bell Centre, Chicago's United Center, or the Wild's Xcel Energy Center, the Devil's home at the Prudential Center ("The Rock") might have the best sight lines in the League. Some suggest that's because no one's sitting in front of you, but in truth, there's not a bad seat. Proof: The inset above was taken from the last row of the nosebleeds. The franchise's proud identity since landing in the Garden State has been challenged, both by its host city and the one 15 miles to the east, casting its long shadow. And though Jersey might seem a world away from the city, it's not; and the cheapest and easiest way to get there is to grab the PATH train from 33rd Street in midtown (near MSG) to Newark Penn Station, and walk a few blocks to the arena. Or take NJ Transit which departs from right beneath the Garden.

PRO PICK

Bryce Salvador
NJ DEVILS '08–'15

EAT / DRINK
HUNTLEY TAVERNE
3 MORRIS AVE., SUMMIT, NJ
908.273.3166

Martin Brodeur
NJ DEVILS '91–'15

Martin Brodeur started in net for one team and held the position for 21 years. Pause on that for a moment. And then check the records: Most wins, shutouts, and games played, along with most goals scored, assists, and points earned by a goalie. Calder Trophy, five Finals, three Cups, four Vezinas. And a statue. But he didn't just dent the record book, he made his mark on the rule book as well. Twice.

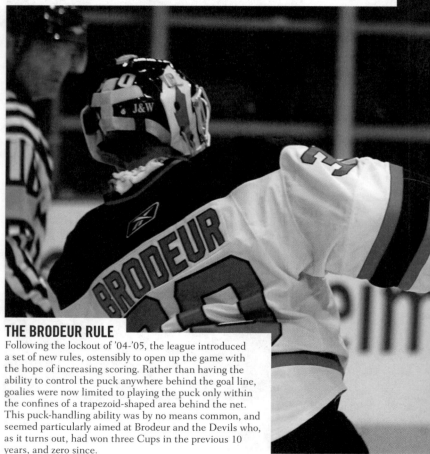

THE BRODEUR RULE

Following the lockout of '04-'05, the league introduced a set of new rules, ostensibly to open up the game with the hope of increasing scoring. Rather than having the ability to control the puck anywhere behind the goal line, goalies were now limited to playing the puck only within the confines of a trapezoid-shaped area behind the net. This puck-handling ability was by no means common, and seemed particularly aimed at Brodeur and the Devils who, as it turns out, had won three Cups in the previous 10 years, and zero since.

THE SEAN AVERY RULE

In a five-on-three power play during game three of the opening round of the 2008 NHL playoffs, Avery, in typical screening fashion, plants himself in front of the net but turns around, facing away from the play (with Jagr blasting from the point), waving his hands and stick in front of an agitated Brodeur. No penalty was called since the move wasn't technically illegal, but it would become so the next day, when the NHL announced a revision to its unsportsmanlike conduct rule—shenanigans like this are a no no. In typical grating irony, Avery scored later on with that same powerplay.

METROPOLITAN RIVETERS

THE BARNABAS HEALTH HOCKEY HOUSE • 25 LAFAYETTE ST., NEWARK, NJ

The National Women's Hockey League has actually solved one of the NHL's unspoken dilemmas: the pro game has reached a critical mass, and by mass we mean size. The stature of NHL players has increased, on average, four inches and 25 pounds since the League's inception a hundred years ago. Simply put, the ice has remained the same, but they're taking up more of it, and since enlarging rinks is out of the question for tens of millions of reasons, the best they've come up with is skating three on three for overtime—arguably a blast to witness, though seen by some as a three-ring gimmick. Enter the women's game. Despite all the setbacks, pivots, and inevitable plan changes, the startup NWHL continues to spread the word that the fairer sex can play this game, and get paid for it, a fact that makes the NWHL unique as the first league to pay women to play hockey. The salaries aren't much, but, in another unique approach, each player receives 15 percent of the profits for any jersey sold with their name on it. In 2016, the New York Riveters made the move from the Aviator Sports Complex in Brooklyn to the Barnabas Health Hockey House (the Devils practice rink in Newark), a smaller venue but one that allows for easier access via mass transit for fans headed to the game from the city. And beginning with the 2017 season, they've struck up an official partnership with the Devils, becoming the Metropolitan Riveters and changing their colors to red and black. Take our word for it: Make the trip, and the first thing you'll notice is how refreshing it is to see talent with some space to operate.

Stan Fischler
LEGENDARY BROADCASTER
& AUTHOR

You don't speak with Stan Fischler so much as have an audience with him, absorbing torrents of knowledge from the past 80 years of NYC history, hockey, and otherwise: people, places, dates, events. The point of our chat was to get a few of his recommendations for the city, which we did eventually get to. Born and raised in a Brooklyn long gone, the man is a speed-walking institution who has truly seen it all.

PREHISTORIC BROOKLYN
I'm three years old, and I see a bunch of guys outside the front of our house digging up Marcy Avenue. "What's going on?" I asked my mom. "They're building the subway," she said, "the new cross-Brooklyn line, the GG line (now the G)."

INTRODUCTION TO HOCKEY
It's 1939, and my father agrees to take me to the Globe Theater on Broadway and 47th Street to see *Snow White and the Seven Dwarves*. We leave Brooklyn, the sun is out, we take the subway, we get to the city, and it's a torrential downpour. My father tells me we're going to the Garden instead, right across the street at 50th and 8th Avenue. The Rangers' farm team, the Rovers, are playing. So we're not going to *Snow White*, but to a hockey game. I'm screaming and crying as he yanks me into the Garden. I'm pissed as hell, I had to get even.

He's rooting for the Rovers? I gotta root for the other team, the Washington Eagles. Normie Burns scores a hat trick and Washington wins, my father's team loses, and I'm feeling pretty good.

A VIOLENT GAME
My Aunt Helen took me to a Rover game. I'm still rooting for the visiting team—in this case, the Philadelphia Falcons. And I used to bring a cowbell to the games. Well, they score, I ring the bell . . . and I whack my Aunt Helen right in the jaw. It was not a good thing.

BLAME IT ON FOSTER HEWITT
For my 10th birthday I got a Philco radio. I start fooling around with the dial, and I hear this voice. It was exciting, and turned out it was the 1942 Cup Final between the Leafs and Red Wings, and it's riveting. I'm hearing names, nicknames, I've never heard before. That Maple Leaf team had the best

nicknames ever in hockey: Wilfred 'Bucko' McDonald, Rudolph "Bingo" Kampman, Walter "Turk" Broader. I was captivated. But it was the broadcaster, Foster Hewitt, the guy who invented hockey broadcasting, and that Final—the Leafs lost the first three and then won four in a row. Never happened before or since. And I became a Leaf fan.

THE TORONTO GLOBE AND MAIL
I'm standing in front of the Paramount Theatre on 43rd St. and Broadway, and I see an out-of-town newsstand across the street. I take a look, and there's a paper from Toronto, 25 cents. "I'll take it." The sports section has all these stories about the Maple Leafs. As soon as I get home, I figure out how to subscribe. From then on, I would get the Toronto Globe and Mail delivered, one day late, to my house in Brooklyn.

THE WALL

In the back of our brownstone, we had a little backyard, and at the end, a brick wall. My parents and grandparents were away for the day. So I went to the hardware store, bought a can of Royal Blue paint. I painted the whole wall white, and, in blue, two crossed sticks and a gigantic Maple Leaf. They all came home. Let's just say they didn't regard it as a Picasso. They were not happy. Years later, after the house was sold and, like the rest of the neighborhood, went to hell, I took a friend of mine for a tour of the old neighborhood, and we drove down Marcy Avenue, and through the rubble of the brownstone, you could see the wall was still there, and my artwork was still there, too.

THE WHIPPETS . . .

The Rangers are playing the Leafs and there's a guy sitting next to me, around my age, rooting for the Leafs—an Irish Catholic kid from Woodside, Queens, named Jimmy Hearndon. He tells me he plays for a roller hockey team called the Woodside Whippets. I had never played for a hockey team, so I ask him, "Can I come out?" and he says sure. I come out, first game, he keeps telling me, "Pay attention." To this day, my producer with the Devils, Roland Dratch, tells me, "Stay focused Fischler, stay focused."

. . . THEN THE WIZARDS

In 1950, I joined the Brooklyn Wizards, a roller hockey team based in Bed Stuy. But instead of playing home games nearby in "The Burg" [Williamsburg], we played home games out on Fort Hamilton Parkway, where there was a Catholic school playground which had a surface that was close to ice. We used quads with Chicago wheels—unless you were poor, then you had Union Hardwares. Five bucks for Chicago, two bucks for Union Hardwares, which, after about a month, they would get "skelleys." Like a car tire, the tred would disappear, like riding on the rims after the rubber wore off. C'mon, find three more bucks, get some Chicagos! The wheels were very thick.

GETTING TO THE GAMES

We're playing our home games on Fort Hamilton—how the hell are we going to get there? One of the guys, Mintz, owned a 1938 DeSoto, six guys max could fit. This thing had no springs, and the challenge was going through Prospect Park—those car lanes were like being on the high seas. Guys were seasick by the time we got there. And we had to bring our own nets. Our goalie, Don Fuhrman, who we called Duck for obvious reasons, built portable nets, Ikea-like, which could be put together when we got there.

WRITING

Mrs. Hochberg, 4th grade, gave the class an assignment: "Write about something." Okay, so I wrote about the life and death of a shoe. She gave me an A, and wrote on it, "You ought to be a writer." Later, I would write a little story about the game on the ticket stubs—the score, maybe six lines worth. I mean, how much could you write on the back of a stub? Then on the game-day programs, I would write entire stories. So I was writing and I knew what I wanted to do. I wanted to write about hockey for a living.

THE TEAMS

Ranger fans need therapy—they're never happy, always worried about something. Devil fans are just enjoying the fact they have a team in their home state, named for their home state. Isles fans, they have the legacy of the Dynasty, and they're devoted and enthused. And, like Ebbets Field, Barclays is an easy place to go to, and from a selfish point of view, I can take the subway. Devils games, I've been lucky over the years to have interns to take me there, or I can take NJ Transit, only 18 minutes.

FAVORITE?

People always ask me "Who do you root for?" I always say, I root for Cablevision, my check *(laughs)*. But seriously, I'd rather go into a happy dressing room than an unhappy dressing room.

BASED IN MONTREAL, IJTEAM PRODUCES HOCKEY JERSEYS FOR BEER LEAGUERS AROUND THE WORLD, INCLUDING THE NYC METRO AREA.

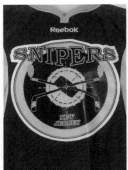

ICE HUTCH
MT. VERNON, NY

WESTCHESTER

WESTCHESTER SKATING ACADEMY
91 FAIRVIEW PARK DR.
ELMSFORD, NY
914.347.8232

HOMMOCKS PARK ICE RINK
140 HOMMOCKS RD.
LARCHMONT, NY
914.834.1069

EJ MURRAY MEMORIAL SKATING CENTER
348 TUCKAHOE RD.
YONKERS, NY
914.377.6469

BREWSTER ICE ARENA
63 FIELDS LN.
BREWSTER, NY
845.279.2229

EVARTS RINK
240 JAY ST.
KATONAH, NY
914.232.8650

PURE HOCKEY
310 MAIN ST.
NEW ROCHELLE, NY
914.278.9210

HUDSON VALLEY HOCKEY COMPANY
250 MAHOPAC AVE.
YORKTOWN HEIGHTS, NY
914.556.6501

PECK'S SKATE & SPORT SHOP
31 LAKE ST.
WHITE PLAINS, NY
914.949.0579

BLUELINE SPORTS WEST
2 HALSTEAD AVE.
HARRISON, NY
914.820.9974

DICK'S SPORTING GOODS
1 MAPLE AVE.
WHITE PLAINS, NY
914.328.3487

45 FITZGERALD ST.
YONKERS, NY
914.964.0580

THE ICE HUTCH
655 GARDEN AVE.
MT VERNON, NY
914.699.6787

EBERSOLE ICE RINK
110 LAKE ST.
WHITE PLAINS, NY
914.422.1390

LONG ISLAND

ICEWORKS SYOSSET
175 UNDERHILL BLVD.
SYOSSET, NY
516.496.2277

PURE HOCKEY
134 E. MAIN ST.
SMITHTOWN, NY
631.982.9440

233 A GLEN COVE RD.
CARLE PLACE, NY
516.742.0471

NORTHWELL HEALTH ICE CENTER AT EISENHOWER PARK
200 MERRICK AVE.
EAST MEADOW, NY
516.441.0070

TOWN OF OYSTER BAY ICE SKATING CENTER
BETHPAGE COMMUNITY PARK
STEWART AND CHERRY AVE.
BETHPAGE, NY

PORT WASHINGTON SKATING CENTER
70 SEAVIEW BLVD.
PORT WASHINGTON, NY
516.484.6800

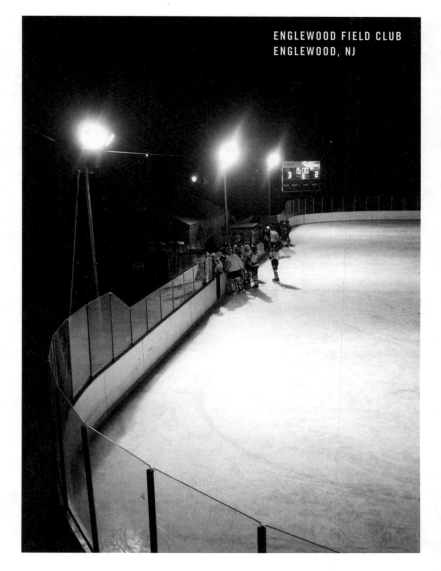

ENGLEWOOD FIELD CLUB
ENGLEWOOD, NJ

FLYERS SKATE ZONE
PENNSAUKEN TOWNSHIP, NJ

PLAY IT AGAIN SPORTS
46 ATLANTIC AVE.
OCEANSIDE, NY
516.678.7900

6160 SUNRISE HWY.
MASSAPEQUA, NY
516.308.4242

HOCKEY SHOP
476 MERRICK RD.
LYNBROOK, NY
516.568.0136

COZZI SPORTS
1001 STEWART AVE.
BETHPAGE, NY
516.719.5959

HOCKEY UNDERGROUND
145 MILBAR BLVD.
FARMINGDALE, NY
631.393.0492

COMLAX
233 A GLEN COVE RD.
CARLE PLACE, NY
516.742.0471

AMITY HARBOR SPORTS
149 MERRICK RD.
AMITYVILLE, NY
631.998.6588

SUPERIOR ICE RINK
270 INDIAN HEAD RD.
KINGS PARK, NY
631.269.3900

LONG BEACH MUNICIPAL ICE ARENA
50 W BAY DR.
LONG BEACH, NY

NEWBRIDGE ARENA
2600 NEWBRIDGE RD.
BELLMORE, NY
516.783.6181

ICELAND
3345 HILLSIDE AVE.
NEW HYDE PARK, NY
516.746.1100

THE RINX
660 TERRY RD.
HAUPPAUGE, NY
631.232.3222

NEW JERSEY

CHARLIE HEGER ICE RINK
807 SUMMIT AVE.
JERSEY CITY, NJ
201.547.4392

RICH KORPI ICE RINK
W 28TH ST.
BAYONNE, NJ
201.858.5566

TOWN OF SECAUCUS ICE RINK
150 PLAZA CENTER
SECAUCUS, NJ
201.330.0273

WARINANCO ICE SKATING CENTER
WARINANCO PARK RDWY.
ROSELLE, NJ
908.298.7850

ICE VAULT ARENA
10 NEVINS RD.
WAYNE, NJ
973.628.1500

PURE HOCKEY
343 RTE 46 W.
FAIRFIELD, NJ
973.287.6720

MONKEYSPORTS SUPERSTORE
1500 ROUTE 9 N.
WOODBRIDGE, NJ
732.634.1446

TWIN OAKS ICE RINK
65 COLUMBIA RD.
MORRISTOWN, NJ
973.292.5699

MONKEYSPORTS SUPERSTORE
WOODBRIDGE, NJ

PROTECHOCKEY PONDS ICE CENTER
15 WORLDS FAIR DR.
SOMERSET, NJ
732.868.9181

IGLOO ICE SKATING RINK
3033 FOSTERTOWN RD.
MT LAUREL, NJ
856.638.0801

MACKAY ICE RINK
130 W ENGLEWOOD AVE.
ENGLEWOOD, NJ
201.568.3133

FLOYD HALL ARENA
MONTCLAIR STATE
UNIVERSITY
28 CLOVE RD.
LITTLE FALLS, NJ
973.746.7744

XHOCKEYPRODUCTS PRO SHOP
FLOYD HALL ARENA
28 CLOVE RD.
LITTLE FALLS, NJ
973.783.2015

UNION SPORTS ARENA,
2441 U.S. 22, UNION, NJ
908.258.0670

BRIDGEWATER SPORTS ARENA
1425 FRONTIER RD.
BRIDGEWATER, NJ

BEACON HILL SKATE SHOP
250 HOBART AVE.
SUMMIT, NJ
908.277.6688

HOCKEY HAUS INC.
410 VOSSELLER AVE.
BOUND BROOK, NJ
732.537.9559

SPORT AND HOUND
1202 VALLEY RD.
STIRLING, NJ
908.580.1188

RICHARD J. CODEY ARENA
560 NORTHFIELD AVE.
WEST ORANGE, NJ
973.731.3828

OCEAN HOCKEY SUPPLY
197 CHAMBERS BRIDGE RD.
BRICK, NJ
732.825.6306

ENGLEWOOD FIELD CLUB
341 ENGLE ST.
ENGLEWOOD, NJ
201.568.0094

BRIDGEWATER SPORTS ARENA
1425 FRONTIER RD.
BRIDGEWATER, NJ
732.627.0006

ICE HOUSE
111 MIDTOWN BRIDGE ST.
HACKENSACK, NJ
201.487.8444

UNION SPORTS ARENA
2441 A US 22
UNION, NJ
908.687.8610

ICE LAND SKATING CENTER
6 TENNIS CT.
HAMILTON TOWNSHIP, NJ
609.588.6672

HOWELL ICE ARENA
269 SQUANKUM RD.
FARMINGDALE, NJ
732.919.7800

SKYLANDS ICE WORLD
2765 NJ-23
STOCKHOLM, NJ
973.697.1600

PRO SKATE
1000 CORNWALL RD.
MONMOUTH JUNCTION, NJ
732.940.6400

CLARY ANDERSON ARENA
41 CHESTNUT ST.
MONTCLAIR, NJ
973.744.6088

CUTTING EDGE ICE ACADEMY
71 MIDLAND AVE.
ELMWOOD PARK, NJ
201.773.6647

FRITZ DIETL ICE SKATING RINK
639 BROADWAY
WESTWOOD, NJ
201.664.9812

BARNABAS HEALTH HOCKEY HOUSE
25 LAFAYETTE ST.
NEWARK, NJ

FLYERS SKATE ZONE
6725 RIVER RD.
PENNSAUKEN TOWNSHIP, NJ
856.488.9300

CONNECTICUT

PURE HOCKEY
677 CONNECTICUT AVE.
NORWALK, CT
203.956.0387

FAIRFIELD ICE ACADEMY
85 MILL PLAIN RD.
FAIRFIELD, CT
203.254.8399

STAMFORD TWIN RINKS
1063 HOPE ST.
STAMFORD, CT
203.968.9000

WINTER GARDEN ICE ARENA
111 PROSPECT RIDGE
RIDGEFIELD, CT
203.438.4423

MILFORD ICE PAVILION
291 BIC DR.
MILFORD, CT
203.878.6516

WONDERLAND OF ICE
123 GLENWOOD AVE.
BRIDGEPORT, CT
203.576.8118

WESTPORT PAL RINK AT LONGSHORE
260 COMPO RD. S.
WESTPORT, CT
203.226.7465

BLUELINE SPORTS AT THE DARIEN ICE RINK
55 OLD KINGS HWY. N.
DARIEN, CT
203.656.0324

SONO ICE HOUSE
300 WILSON AVE.
NORWALK, CT
203.956.0255

CHELSEA PIERS CONNECTICUT
1 BLACHLEY RD.
STAMFORD, CT
203.989.1000

DANBURY ICE ARENA
1 INDEPENDENCE WAY
DANBURY, CT
203.794.1704

TERRY CONNERS ICE RINK
1125 COVE RD.
STAMFORD, CT
203.977.4514

WINTER GARDEN ICE ARENA
49 CHESTNUT WOODS RD.
REDDING, CT
203.438.4423

DARIEN ICE HOUSE
55 OLD KINGS HWY. N.
DARIEN, CT
203.655.8251

SPORTS CENTER OF CONNECTICUT
784 RIVER RD.
SHELTON, CT
203.929.6500

DOROTHY HAMILL SKATING RINK
14 SHERMAN AVE.
GREENWICH, CT
203.531.8560

FERGUSON'S CENTER ICE SPORTS
307 RACEBROOK RD.
ORANGE, CT
203.799.7200

FAIRFIELD'S SPORTS
85 MILL PLAIN RD.
FAIRFIELD, CT
203.292.9396

HOCKEY HANGERS
36 WALLACKS DR.
STAMFORD, CT
203.998.6450

1

HERSHEYPARK ARENA (1)
100 W. HERSHEYPARK DR.
HERSHEY, PA

BRIDGEPORT SOUND TIGERS
WEBSTER BANK ARENA
600 MAIN ST.
BRIDGEPORT, CT
203.334.4625

HARTFORD WOLFPACK
XL CENTER
1 CIVIC CENTER PLAZA
HARTFORD, CT
860.249.6333

HOBEY BAKER MEMORIAL RINK
132 UNIVERSITY PL.
PRINCETON TOWNSHIP, NJ
609.258.4466

INGALLS RINK YALE UNIVERSITY
73 SACHEM ST.
NEW HAVEN, CT
203.432.0876

RYE PLAYLAND
1 PLAYLAND PKWY.
RYE, NY
914.813.7010

TATE RINK WEST POINT
US MILITARY ACADEMY MILLS RD.
WEST POINT, NY
845.938.4481

SPRINGFIELD THUNDERBIRDS
MASSMUTUAL CENTER
45 BRUCE LANDON WAY
SPRINGFIELD, MA
413.739.4625

WESCO SPORTS CENTER
270 FEDERAL RD.
BROOKFIELD, CT
203.775.2227

Danny Blanda [1]
PLAYWRIGHT

Despite growing up in Atlanta, I was raised to be a devout New York Rangers fan (though I still mourn the loss of the Atlanta Thrashers, having skated through their youth-development programs). I write for theater and film, and currently work for Westside Skate and Stick in the Flatiron District.

Mikhail Bortnik [2]
FOUNDER, MISHKA NYC

Honorary Beer Leaguer

I'm like most sports fans: The team I root for is the one my family (my dad in this case) rooted for. Why the Devils? For the longest time I really assumed my dad picked the Devils because we were Russian, and they were among the first NHL teams to bring over Russian players—Fetisov in particular—but that wasn't until '89, and I realized I had been watching or listening to Devils games before that. So I asked my dad, who informed me that he chose the Devils as his team over the Rangers and Islanders because at the time they were brand new. Moving to the area only a few years after my parents immigrated to the US, the Devils came with no baggage. Ranger fans were obnoxious, and the Islanders were just coming out of a Dynasty. Plus, Devils tix were cheaper and easier to get. Growing up, I went to almost as many Islanders games as Devils games. I loved Lafontaine, Turgeon, and consider Ziggy Palffy one of my favorite players ever. And unlike the Rangers (who we despised), we liked the Islanders as long as they weren't playing the Devils. But the Devils were always the underdogs (even in '95) for most of my adolescence. They had an awesome name . . . and one of the slickest logos in all of sports. And, of course, the Russians.

Jack Chinelli [3]
SNIPETOWN EDITOR

As a New York City native, I grew up playing travel ice hockey throughout the Hudson Valley. When roller hockey was heating up, I was just hitting my teenage years and joining pick-up games with friends in Soho, where we'd skate against traffic into Paragon Sports, skates on, to ask if they had balls. Street hockey balls that is.

Brian Curtin [4]
DEVELOPER

I played hockey a bit as a kid, then life happened, and after about a 10-year break, I came back to the sport playing pick-up games in Chicago. After moving to Brooklyn, I found my way onto the roster of Snipetown and am now the team's captain. Victories have been few and far between, but I'll keep putting on that sweater as long as we keep having fun. Off the ice, software development pays the bills, and photography clears my mind. The best times though are spent with my little family: a loving girlfriend and a loving dog.

Mike Dudolevitch [5]
MUSICIAN

Growing up we lived on a cul-de-sac that made a perfect spot for pick-up street hockey games, and all the other kids in the neighborhood would play every weekend. A couple of us that played as little kids stuck with it and played together in random leagues and through high school. I met Trevor Tyrell, formerly of the Dark Rainbows (BTSH team), at Mulholland's during a Capitals-Rangers game. We were both wearing Caps jerseys, and naturally started talking. He asked if I played at all and mentioned that his street hockey team could use another guy, then pointed me in the direction of how to sign up.

Colin Earyes [6]
BARTENDER

I play for the Hoyt Hooligans and Harvey Wednesdays. I live in Astoria, originally from Scranton, PA. When I first moved to NYC I would usually go to a park near my apartment late at night after work and shoot into a can for an hour or so. It wouldn't be odd for me to go for a skate at 2 or 3 a.m. My third year in NYC I moved to Astoria, and on Memorial Day I was walking home and happened to have my gear on me. I passed by Hoyt Park, and there was a pick-up game going on. I asked if they minded having an additional player. They welcomed me, and I am still skating with the same group every Sunday now three years later!

7

8

9

Jason Faustino [7]
CREATIVE DIRECTOR

The straight-edge beer leaguer. As a co-founder at Extra Butter, I was able to bring my worlds together working on a project where we designed a limited-edition sneaker—Reebok Ventilator Supreme for the New York Islanders. It was a big step in a lifetime spent slowly crawling closer and closer to the sport I loved, finally getting on the ice and learning how to play this game at the late age of 37. I proudly wear an "A" for a struggling new team called the "Seige." Hockey keeps my mind and body healthy, creative, and motivated in my work world. I enjoy the brotherhood and the lessons learned on ice that translate to life—not to mention, all the gear and styling up to be the best beaut I can be.

Andre Legaspi [8]
WRITER

As a kid, I gummed up my bearings skating in every roller-hockey rink in Queens. After college, my itinerant nature eventually led me to write for Frommer's and Travel Channel. I am currently a freelance photographer with work that's been exhibited in the Museum of Flight, the Astoria Historical Society, and on my father's refrigerator door. When time allows, I play in a beer league in LIC, ball hockey in the Lower East Side, roller hockey in Astoria and Whitestone, and pond hockey tournaments in Wisconsin and upstate New York.

Jim Lester [9]
VENUE MANAGER

I play with the Scottsmen at City Ice Pavilion. The first few years I lived in the city, I couldn't afford to play in any of the leagues. Eventually I threw my name on the City Ice Free Agents list and Jason Hasday reached out to ask me to join his Lasker team for the winter 2014 season. Since then, I've been playing for the Scotts at City Ice. I've gone through the curriculum at the Upright Citizens Brigade Theater and manage their bars, so their Chelsea and East Village theaters are always high on my list when it comes to seeing improvised comedy live.

10

11

12

Briton Malcomson [10]

BIKE MECHANIC

I'm from the Philadelphia suburbs. My father played hockey before I was born so there was hockey equipment in the house growing up, and I used to play street hockey with my cousins. Some of my childhood friends played ice hockey, but I never even learned how to skate until much later. A good friend of mine got me back into watching hockey a few years ago, and then, in 2015, I decided to try and learn to play. I've been a bike mechanic for nine years and worked at Citibike for four years. I currently co-own a bicycle maintenance and delivery cooperative called Workers Transport.

Daniel Seely [11]

MUSICIAN

When not on the ice for various beer league teams, I'm the frontman for a Long Island hardcore band called King Nine. My recommendation: If you want to play hockey, you need to be on Long Island, just for the access to rinks (but NYC has their share of rinks too). Enjoy your stay in the jungle.

Melody Tran [12]

EDUCATOR

I'm a special education teacher by day and a beer leaguer/bench-warming enthusiast by night. I work in a special needs elementary school in Queens, teaching children in 3rd, 4th, and 5th grade who cope with moderate-to-severe or multiple disabilities. I started playing hockey to fulfill a lifelong dream of learning how to play, and I haven't looked back since. I play with the New York City Gay Hockey Association as an ally and participate in two different leagues at Chelsea Piers.

ACKNOWLEDGMENTS

Thanks to Ann Treistman and the crew at The Countryman Press for thinking this book might work. For all their help in putting this guide together, acknowledgment goes out to Brian Curtin, Andre Legaspi, Jason Faustino, Calvin Burkhart, Danny Blanda, Jack Chinelli, Chris Cosentino, Andrew Link, Melody Tran, John Sanful, Bruce Bennett, Stan Fischler, Fluto Shinzawa, and Jaimie Korelitz at Getty Images. For putting up with me during the production of this book, acknowledgment goes out to the family: JBS, MSG, and TRG.

PHOTO CREDITS

INDEX

Italics indicate illustrations.

INDEX

INDEX

INDEX